BEYOND SMELLS & BELLS

THE WONDER AND POWER OF CHRISTIAN LITURGY

MARK GALLI

PARACLETE PRESS

BREWSTER, MASSACHUSETTS

Beyond Smells and Bells: The Wonder and Power of Christian Liturgy

2008 First Printing

Copyright © 2008 by Mark Galli

ISBN: 978-1-55725-521-1

Library of Congress Cataloging-in-Publication Data

Galli, Mark.
  Beyond smells and bells : the wonder and power of Christian liturgy /
by Mark Galli.
      p. cm.
  ISBN 978-1-55725-521-1
  1. Liturgics. 2. Public worship. I. Title.
  BV176.3.G35 2008
  264--dc22   2008000737

10 9 8 7 6 5 4 3 2 1

Published by Paraclete Press
Brewster, Massachusetts
www.paracletepress.com
Printed in the United States of America

CONTENTS

INTRODUCTION

*And we all with unveiled face, beholding the glory
of the Lord, are being transformed into
the same image from one degree of glory to another.*
—ST. PAUL

I WRITE THIS BOOK FOR THOSE WHO FIND THEMSELVES
ATTRACTED TO LITURGY but don't quite know why. For
those immersed in liturgy and want to think more deeply
about it. And for those who wonder if it is worth committing
themselves to a liturgical church. The book is an attempt to
explain how liturgy shapes us as we participate in it week after
week, year after year.

The readers I hope will enjoy this book are those in or
exploring Anglican, Presbyterian, Methodist, Lutheran, and
Roman Catholic churches. (While the book should also have
meaning for those exploring Eastern Orthodoxy, the Orthodox
liturgy is too complex to be an entry point to liturgy, so I mostly
use examples from the Western liturgies. Still, readers will note
my dependence on Orthodox theology and writing, especially
that of Alexander Schmemann, and especially his *For the Life of
the World: Sacraments and Orthodoxy.*)

We live in a spiritually restless culture. Some twelve million
Americans are active participants in, and another thirty
million are intrigued by, alternative spiritual systems. In the
twentieth century, somewhere between 1,000 to 2,000 new

religious movements were formed in the United States. This gives American religious life a unique character—as sociologist Wayne Roof put it, "an eclectic mix of religious and spiritual ideas and practices."

Since the days of the Puritans, Americans have had an irresistible impulse to create a uniquely personal spirituality, experimenting with divination, astrology, witchcraft, angelology, Swedenborgianism, transcendentalism, New Thought and New Age, and various forms of psychotherapy, seeking both experiential and ritualized faith.

Running parallel with this trend has been another, one that has been quiet and steadily growing as well: an ongoing fascination with orthodoxy, tradition, and the lasting rituals of the Christian faith. Colleen Carroll Campbell describes how and why young adults continue to be attracted to the traditional liturgy. In her book, *The New Faithful: Why Young Adults Are Embracing Christian Orthodoxy,* she says, "The benefits far surpass those of psychotherapy, chats with friends, even private prayer. For them, the sacraments and devotions of the institutional church allow them to be cleansed, healed, and strengthened. For young adults . . .these rites offer something so powerful that they weep in the face of it, so irresistible that they cannot walk away from it."

A move toward informal and spontaneous worship is clearly a world trend (as witnessed by the growth of Pentecostalism), yet at the same time, the majority of Christians in the world today are Roman Catholics, Orthodox, Anglicans, and high-church Protestants in mainline churches. The liturgy—whose basic outline is the same in all these traditions—remains the staple of Sunday worship and daily prayer for millions for a reason: it allows people to enter into an enduring story that makes sense of life, and allows them to enter into communion with God in a way that touches body, mind, and soul. So it's no surprise that an increasing number of low-church evangelicals are exploring liturgical worship, as well.

In this book, I try to show how the liturgy helps us enter a *counter-intuitive* story. In an individualistic culture, the liturgy helps us live a communal life. In a culture that values spontaneity, the liturgy grounds us in something enduring. In a culture that assumes that truth is a product of the mind, the liturgy helps us experience truth in both mind and body. In a world demanding instant relevance, the liturgy gives us the patience to live into a relevance that the world does not know. Its counter-intuitive nature makes the liturgy appear culturally strange at first, but in fact it's more like an intriguing story, full of mystery, that not only attracts but reshapes our perceptions and our lives.

A caution. The liturgy is not a magic potion or carpet ride. The dreariest services I've been to have been liturgical services. And the spiritually deadest churches I've attended have been rich in liturgy. When that is the case, I understand why the radical reformers rejected not only medieval Catholic doctrine but also Catholic worship—they found little life in the Spirit compared to their free-form services.

But there is a reason the liturgy has continued to be the staple of the bulk of Christendom: it remains a powerful context in which to meet and be transformed by God. Still, it should not surprise us that the liturgy is also one of the best places to hide from God. The Garden of Eden was a place where Adam and Eve enjoyed the goodness of God and hid from his presence.

Yet if we will refuse to hide within the ritual, it can work on us and in us to transform us. I believe—and it has been my experience—that ongoing participation in the liturgy is ongoing participation in the life of God and, as such, will lead, as C.S. Lewis envisions human transformation, to a life "dazzling, radiant . . . pulsating all through with . . . energy, joy, and wisdom and love as we cannot now imagine."

CHAPTER 1

LIVING THE OLD, OLD STORY

The Basic Outline of the Liturgy

THE LITURGY LIVES OUT A STORY IN A STORY-DEPRIVED WORLD. Liturgy is not a once-upon-a-time story we merely watch others perform. We are the characters in this story, actors in the divine drama whose opening and closing has been written by Jesus Christ himself.

The story that modernity gave us has had its run. Its story arc was about progress, the notion that human life would get better and better because science and technology would solve the most nagging human problems. But events—two world wars, the Gulags, the holocaust, HIV/AIDS, and 9/11—and postmodern philosophy have revealed how weak this plot line was. Only the most hopeless romantics remain fascinated with it.

The failure of this story touches us personally, because we breathe the air of despair daily. We find it difficult to give ourselves to anything larger than the self; we simply don't trust anymore—not government, not business, not even the church. So we give our energy to career and comfort, to family and a few friends. We collapse into a cocoon of meaning, realizing in our more lucid moments that our little cocoon has no meaning larger than the self.

The liturgy speaks to us at this point. The liturgy is lucidity inducing. When we participate in it, even if we don't understand 90 percent of what is going on, we recognize intuitively how small our lives are, that the story we've concocted for ourselves is but a child's nursery rhyme—and that we are being beckoned to enter a drama that is epic in scope.

Liturgy comes from a Greek word meaning "a public service." When I refer to "the liturgy" in this book, I am referring to the public Sunday service performed by liturgical and mainline churches. I refer to it in the singular because the shape of the service is remarkably similar in all these traditions (see Appendix B).

Sometimes by *liturgy* I mean something wider in scope: the body of prayers and services that make up the whole life of a church—from daily prayer to Good Friday services to weddings and funerals. Many of these prayers and services can be found in more than one church tradition, while others are unique to only one. But overall these extra-Sunday services share the same larger characteristics of the public Sunday services that will be described in this book—especially a grounding in history and tradition that remains immediately relevant in paradoxical and mysterious ways.

Though different traditions divide the Sunday service in different ways with different terms, one common way is to think of the service, and the story it embodies, as having four "acts": *Gathering, Word, Sacrament, Dismissal.* As we proceed, we'll see that the story is richer than this simple outline, because the liturgy contains a story within a story. It tells a story. It enacts a story. It is an episode in an unfolding story. But these four acts are at the heart of the larger story told within the liturgy.

The service begins with the *Gathering,* which is so much more than an efficient way to get things started. This part of the service points us back to God's gathering the people of Israel to himself:

> Let the redeemed of the LORD say so,
>> whom he has redeemed from trouble
> and gathered in from the lands,
>> from the east and from the west,
>> from the north and from the south.

In the same way, the opening reminds us of God's gathering a people in Jesus Christ, symbolized in the calling of the twelve disciples to himself. The Gathering also points forward to the day when God will gather all those he has chosen to gather (who have not rejected his invitation) in a great festal celebration, as Isaiah said,

> On this mountain the LORD of hosts will make for all peoples
>> a feast of rich food, a feast of well-aged wine,
>> of rich food full of marrow, of aged wine well refined.

The Gathering is no small thing.

The Gathering usually begins with the congregation singing a hymn, the joining together of all voices. This is a concrete, embodied way to signal that we are gathering as one people, not as a collection of individuals. Then comes the opening acclamation in the service:

> Blessed be God: Father, Son, and Holy Spirit.
> And blessed be his kingdom, now and forever!

We will return to this opening response time and again in this book, because it signals so much of what is happening in the liturgy. For now, note how in the Gathering, we are already being pointed to the grand climax of the Christian story, having been gathered in a concrete way by a God whose very history has been to gather a people to himself.

The service then moves into the portion called the *Word*, the focus of which is the reading of Scripture. The Word is one of the two centers of the liturgy (so much so, that some liturgies describe the service as having just two parts: Word and Sacrament).

In a typical liturgical service, three Scripture passages are read each week: one from the Old Testament, one from the Pauline or General Epistles, and one from the Gospels. The service also includes the reading of a psalm. These readings are arranged in a three-year cycle so that we hear the entire biblical story: the Creation and the Fall, the Exodus, the Captivity and return, the promise and then the Advent of the Messiah, the coming of the Holy Spirit, and the promise of the coming kingdom.

The meaning of the biblical story unfolds week by week in the sermon, which follows immediately after the Scripture readings. This order signals that the sermon is grounded, not on the morning news or the book-of-the month, but on the biblical story. Following the sermon, the biblical story is summarized as we read the Creed, which structures the story in three movements—Father, Son, and Holy Spirit.

In the "act" called *Sacrament*, we partake of bread and wine in a ritual that is sometimes called "Communion" or "Eucharist."

Before the partaking of bread and wine, the story is rehearsed in the Eucharistic prayer. This longer prayer reminds us about God's work in creation, fall, redemption, Pentecost, and the Second Coming. At the heart of this act is the participation in a great feast, the sharing of bread and wine. The bread and wine point back to the death and the Resurrection of Jesus Christ, and forward to his coming again. Thus by sharing this meal, we remember the whole sweep of our story.

This core of a liturgical service helps us remember symbolically our history and theology as a people, but more crucially, it is also the moment when Christ becomes present for us in a mysterious but remarkable way. Thus many books on the meaning of the liturgy rightly spend much time mining its depths. This book will not follow this pattern, because I want to highlight other aspects of the liturgy, as well. But if the liturgy is a story, the Eucharist is certainly the climax of that story, the larger story embedded in the liturgical story.

Similar to the Gathering, the *Dismissal* at the conclusion of the service is not merely a convenient way to get people out the door. During the Dismissal, we say a prayer asking God to send us out "to do the work you have given us to do." What is that work? To participate with God in calling out a people to be co-workers in God's great gathering mission, the same mission Isaiah felt deep in his spirit:

And now the LORD says,
    he who formed me from the womb to be his servant,
to bring Jacob back to him;
    and that Israel might be gathered to him. . . .

So, the liturgy teaches us *about* the story, especially in Word and Sacrament. But it does more. It also *embodies* the Christian story in its very structure—God gathers people for a great banquet at which he presides, gives us a Word, and offers us the fruit of his labor of love. From there, God sends us out to participate in the great gathering work.

By participating in the liturgy, we're doing more than "attending a service." We are entering a story—a story in which we also play a role. We are the people who have indeed been gathered. We are the people who share in God's very life. We are the people sent forth to proclaim God's story and to invite people into the grand story.

The dramatic sweep of the liturgical story is summarized well by Father Jeremy Driscoll:

> The meaning of the whole creation and the whole of human history is contained here in ritual form and in the people who enact the ritual. This action will cause the Church to be: to do Eucharist is to be Church. To be Church, to be assembled into one, is what God intends for the world. The Eucharist is celebrated in thanksgiving and for the glory of God, and it is done for the salvation of the whole world.

For people who find themselves storyless, or with a story that has no larger meaning than the self, the liturgy is a salvation. It shows that we do not have to abandon hope; we don't have to fabricate a new myth to force meaning onto the world. We can participate in the very story of God—Father, Son, and Holy

Spirit—who has created and redeemed us, who has gathered us to himself already in a Great Feast, and who promises, in the last act, to gather all things on heaven and earth to himself, so that we may feast together for eternity.

CHAPTER 2

COSMIC DAYTIMER
*How the Liturgical Calendar Can Bring Order
to Our Lives*

T HE PROFESSOR BEGAN OUR GRADUATE SEMINAR in
historiography with a simple question: "Does anyone
know what happened on October 3, 1951?"

I looked around the table at the eight other graduate students
in history. We were studying at the University of California
at Davis, just eighty miles from Candlestick Park, then home
of the San Francisco Giants. Surely someone knew what the
professor was talking about. But only blank stares responded.
So I spoke up.

"That was the day Bobby Thompson hit 'the shot heard
round the world.'"

"Yes," the professor replied. "Tell us about it."

"Well, the New York Giants were behind the Brooklyn
Dodgers 4-2, and it was the bottom of the ninth inning. The
Giants had been eleven and a half games behind the Dodgers in
early August but had caught them by the end of the season to tie
for first place. This was the third game of the resulting playoffs,
the teams having split the first two games. Bobby Thompson
was up to bat with two runners on. A nervous rookie, Willie
Mays, was in the on-deck circle. Thompson was facing Ralph
Branca, who ironically, was wearing number thirteen.

"Branca threw a fastball for a called strike, followed by another
pitch 'up-and-in' to intimidate Thompson. Didn't work. Next

pitch was another fastball, which Thompson hit over the left field fence. The Giants won the pennant in one of the greatest comebacks, both in terms of a season and a single game, in the history of baseball."

The professor replied, "Very good," and the rest of the students just stared at me in awe. They wondered how I knew all that. More to the point, *why* did I know all that?

I knew because as a boy I had immersed myself in the story of the New York and then San Francisco Giants, and I lived by baseball time. The Giants were my saints, and the year was marked not by winter, spring, summer, and fall, but by spring training, opening day, All-Star break, and the World Series. The Giants gave order and meaning to my childhood.

Baseball is like many of the stories that overlay our lives, each with their own saints and sense of time. Like these other stories, the baseball story is but a shadow of the larger story that overlays our world, a story with saints of an extraordinary nature, and a calendar that marks time for eternity. This calendar is called the liturgical calendar, or the Christian calendar.

I began writing this chapter in earnest during the feast of the Nativity of John the Baptist, better known in our culture as June 24. The church season of Pentecost was well underway, but in secular time, summer was just beginning.

This dual way of understanding time is at the very heart of the liturgy. Some think liturgical timekeeping—that is, the liturgical calendar—is merely a throwback to the Middle Ages, when the whole of Christendom lived by the church calendar. In our day, a scientifically precise age, when watches keep time to the hundredth of a second, this sounds all ancient and quaint—

a nice devotional reminder, but not relevant to daily life. The liturgical calendar doesn't help us know how to dress before we step out the door—a warm coat or shorts and sandals—or how to regulate our work or school schedules.

But the liturgy is not spiritual entertainment for antiquarians. The church calendar aims at nothing less than to change the way we experience time and perceive reality.

For the church, January 1 is not all that significant. Neither is September, the start of school for most of us in the West, although it may feel like the start of a "new year." For the church, Advent signals the new year. For the church, the annual rhythm is not winter, spring, summer, and fall, but Advent, Christmas, Epiphany, Lent, Easter, and Pentecost (what some traditions call Ordinary time—see Appendix C for a more detailed explanation of the church year). The church calendar is not about the cycle of life—school or sports or harvest time— but about the movement of history toward a glorious goal. We celebrate the past events of salvation history not merely to remember them, but to note how they infuse the present with meaning and power, and point us to our future hope.

Select any day of the year, and you can find its liturgical significance, and therefore deeply Christian sense—for instance, the Nativity of John the Baptist on June 24. It is not a mere coincidence that the church established this day almost six months to the day from the Nativity of Jesus Christ, Christmas. For from time of the birth of John the Baptist, the forerunner of the Messiah, the preacher of repentance, until the time of the Savior's birth, the daylight gets shorter and shorter, the light of the world seems to be dying. From the birth of our Lord onward, daylight grows, with light permeating more and more of daily life.

The liturgical calendar, therefore, causes us to think of June 24 primarily as the Nativity of John the Baptist, not the beginning of summer but a turning point in our year, when we already begin to look forward to the coming of Jesus.

In many places in the northern hemisphere, Lent begins just as spring is emerging. It is counterintuitive to start thinking about repentance and fasting, just when the world around us is coming to life. Yet the liturgical calendar reminds us that this earth is not our home, that in the midst of the glories of spring, we must not forget the tragedy and frustration that now marks this world.

> April is the cruelest month, breeding
> Lilacs out of the dead land, mixing
> Memory and desire, stirring
> Dull roots with spring rain.

It is no surprise that Anglo-Catholic T.S. Eliot, deeply imbued with a sense of liturgical time, could perceive this paradox of spring.

We cannot ignore the calendar that the rest of the world lives by. This calendar we can call the cosmic calendar because it takes it cues from the cosmos, the movement of the moon and of the earth in relation to the sun. It is an efficient and accurate way to measure the passing of time. More importantly, the cosmic calendar is the result of God's creativity: "And God said, 'Let there be lights in the expanse of the heavens to separate the day from the night. And let them be for signs and for seasons, and for days and years.'"

The cosmic calendar is also God's gift. Once we figured out how to measure it—from the sundial to mechanical clocks, to digital and atomic clocks—we have become increasingly precise. This makes possible efficient airline travel, a host of medical miracles, instant messaging, and online banking. Not something to lift one's nose at, the cosmic calendar enables us to structure our years, weeks, days, and minutes.

Efficiency, in fact, characterizes our world; it defines and shapes our culture. We are people who live by the clock, and we measure success and happiness by our ability to manipulate time. We strive to "save" time, meaning we use the passing of time as a standard to measure whether something has been done well. It is no accident that in a culture ruled by this calendar and clock, efficiency is an intrinsic goal, not something one has to justify or defend.

There *is* something right and good about celebrating the seasons as such—spring bursting forth in new life, the gloriously lazy pace of summer, the beautiful death of fall, and the cold winter when we huddle together to find warmth.

Because this sense of time has indeed been created by God, it is in many ways "good," just as he said. This is why, while recognizing the supremacy of the liturgical calendar, the church has never thought of forsaking the cosmic calendar, and in fact, uses the cosmic calendar as the basis of the liturgical calendar. The date of Easter, after all, has little to do with the actual day on which Jesus rose from the grave, because it is the first Sunday after the first full moon on or after the spring equinox.

This becomes just one more point in the liturgical life where we see Incarnation at work. Before he became pope, Benedict XVI put it this way:

> Cosmic time, which is determined by the sun, becomes a representation of human time and of historical time, which moves toward union of God and the world, of history and the universe, of matter and spirit—in a word, toward the New City whose light is God himself. Thus time becomes eternity, and eternity is imparted to time.

Or more simply, and more to the point: "In the Son, time co-exists with eternity."

And so with those who believe in Jesus. We are in the world, but not of it. We are citizens of the kingdom that transcends time, but we sojourn on a time-bound earth. We are the people who, in the same breath, pray "thy kingdom come" and "give us this day our daily bread."

Without liturgical time, we can easily forget our eternal identity. Without our cosmic calendar, we'd be so kingdom-minded, we would be of no historical good.

> "I do not ask that you take them out of the world, but that you keep them from the evil one. They are not of the world, just as I am not of the world. Sanctify them in the truth; your word is truth. As you sent me into the world, so I have sent them into the world."

The same tension is juxtaposed in the liturgy. This tension starts with the naming of the Sunday on which we worship—the second Sunday in Advent or the fifth Sunday of Pentecost. It continues through the lectionary readings, which are based on the liturgical season we find ourselves in. And it is expressed in the prayers, like the prayer after the Eucharist, when we pray, "We are . . heirs of your *eternal kingdom*. And *now send us out* to do the work you have given us to do."

While both time and eternity must continue to intersect, the meaning of time is determined by eternity. That's why the meaning of the liturgical year will sometimes differ in the Southern Hemisphere, where Lent, for example, occurs in what is its fall season. The season seems to reinforces the sense of Lent's preoccupation with repentance and death of the self. Easter season ends as its winter begins and light fades, reminding the church there that resurrection life is lived in the midst of a dark world.

So the meaning of any day or year is not determined by the cosmic calendar alone, nor the liturgical calendar alone, but by a dance between the two, with the liturgical calendar taking the lead.

"So teach us to number our days," says the psalmist, "that we may get a heart of wisdom." By *number* the psalmist is not just talking about realizing how short our lives are and making them count. He also encourages us to note the significance of our days, which is why some translations read, "teach us to order our days." Ordering our days brings wisdom not only in the sense of teaching us to live faithfully before we die. It also brings us into a relationship with Wisdom. Only in the light of Jesus

Christ can we see the deeper meaning of this little verse—that wisdom would become incarnate in Jesus Christ, and that by ordering our days by both the cosmic and liturgical calendars, we would learn to experience both time and eternity.

CHAPTER 3

LIFE TOGETHER
How the Liturgy Draws Us into Community

MY WIFE, BARBARA, AND I once sat down to a meal with her aunt and uncle, devout Roman Catholics. Barbara's aunt asked her to say grace, and Barbara prayed in words that came to her at the moment.

When we lifted our heads, her aunt said, "Barb, I just love it when you pray. You talk to Jesus as if he were your friend."

God is indeed our friend. That means God listens with rapt attention no matter how confused the words are that come dribbling out of our mouths.

But during one period in my prayer life, when I turned to God each morning, my prayers seemed less like sincere, simple utterings to a friend. I felt increasingly inadequate and alone. God's presence was still real at times, and I didn't doubt God's love or life's meaning. But when I praised God, my language fell appallingly short of the glory God deserved. My prayers of confession did not suggest the depth of my culpability or remorse. My petitions for loved ones felt trivial.

I longed to offer more than banalities, but banalities were all that emerged from my solitary soul.

One day not long after that season of loneliness, I bumped into the liturgy. On the advice of a friend, I decided to try out the Book of Common Prayer in an attempt to order my morning prayers.

"Blessed be God: Father, Son, and Holy Spirit," I read toward the beginning of the liturgy (in the section I've called the Gathering). "And blessed be his kingdom, now and forever." Next came the great prayer called Glory to God, or The Gloria, which proclaims the majesty of the Trinitarian God and ends like this:

> For you alone are the Holy One,
> you alone are the Lord,
> you alone are the Most High,
> Jesus Christ,
> with the Holy Spirit,
> in the glory of God the Father. Amen.

I noticed that prayers throughout this liturgical symphony returned again and again to the Trinitarian theme, often addressing God "through Jesus Christ our Lord, to whom, with you and the Holy Spirit, be honor and glory throughout all ages. Amen."

These words, or ones very much like them, begin the liturgy of all the major traditions. They take us into a strange world, one that is not about the self, which so easily becomes banal, but about a glorious God. Not about a solitary, dispassionate God who lives in peaceful isolation within his own perfections, but a God who from eternity has "lived in community" as Father, Son, and Holy Spirit.

For me, this was the first hint that the liturgy might be the cure for spiritual loneliness.

Though I felt inadequate and alone during my prayer crisis, I was not alone. Much of American spiritual life trudges through the muck of solitary spirituality.

Twenty years ago, Robert Bellah described this phenomenon in *Habits of the Heart,* with his now famous description of one woman:

> Sheila Larson is a young nurse who has received a good deal of therapy and describes her faith as "Sheilaism." This suggests the logical possibility of more than 235 million American religions, one for each of us. "I believe in God," Sheila says. "I am not a religious fanatic. I can't remember the last time I went to church. My faith has carried me a long way. It's Sheilaism. Just my own little voice."

"My little voice" guides many lonely people to and through New Age, wicca, Buddhism, labyrinths, Scientology, yoga, meditation, and various fads in Christianity—and then creates a new Sheilaism from the fragments that have not been discarded along the way.

I love Sheila Larson precisely because she articulates nearly perfectly my lifelong struggle: "I believe in God. I am not a religious fanatic. . . . My faith has carried me a long way. It's Sheilism. Just my own little voice." The difference between Sheila and me is that she has the courage of her convictions: she knows her faith is very personal and so hasn't bothered with the church. I like to pretend that my faith is grounded in community, but I struggle to believe in anything but Markism.

Fortunately God loves us so much he has made it a "spiritual law" that Sheilism or Markism become boring after awhile. The gift of the liturgy—and it is precisely why I *need* the liturgy—is that it helps me hear not so much "my little voice" but instead the still, small voice (Psalm 46). It leads away from the self and points me toward the community of God.

The liturgy leads us first to the Triune God. In the beginning was God, and that means in the beginning was relationship—between Father, Son, and Holy Spirit. We do not worship a solitary "monogod," sufficient unto himself, but one who has existed from eternity in self-giving love among the members of the Trinity.

If God-as-Trinity is the core reality of the universe, that means that the core of reality is community.

This is not easy for someone like me to accept. I have been suckled since infancy on the metaphor of the social contract: we are individuals first who then band together when it serves our self-interest. The community exists to help me self-actualize. I take it or leave it depending on whether it helps me do that. So I never really commit to community.

My lifelong participation in the church seems to belie that, but I've learned the fine art of participating without being fully present, of doing a flurry of work for the church but hiding my deeper self from others. I never get deeply involved in the lives of others, because, well, that just complicates my life. It is a fearful thing to fall into the hands of a living community.

I'd like to think that I can manage life on my own, with just a *little* help from friends—as long as I keep my emotional distance. My primary identity, I like to imagine, is wrapped up in my gifts and talents and unique characteristics—as if the essence of my being is the "I," making the "we" of community a nice add-on, but not necessary. But the truth is that the core of my identity lies not in my individuality. Locke, Hobbes, and Rousseau notwithstanding, it is not "I think, therefore I am." It is not, like Sheila, "I believe, therefore I am." The deeper truth is this: "God speaks, therefore we are."

Or as the author of Genesis put it, "Let *us* create man in our image"—in the image of a Trinity of persons we have been created.

"And he created humankind, male and female he created them"—and thus human existence is pictured as triune: man-woman-God. This is an icon of human community into which God has created us. Though fragmented and broken at this stage in history, it is nonetheless the community to which we are again headed: "Blessed be his kingdom now and forever."

The liturgy is a story we participate in. Part of that story is the story of community—created, broken, and restored.

This story is both liberating (freeing us from the burden of the self) and utterly frightening (we have to step out of the self). But this is the God and the community that the liturgy wants us to meet—and be transformed by.

Yikes!

The liturgy comes to us in many forms. There are liturgies for Sunday worship, and liturgies for special days, like Ash Wednesday and Good Friday. There are also daily liturgies that one can pray with others or alone. The paradox of these daily liturgies is that we never pray alone despite praying by ourselves. In saying the prayers of the Book of Common Prayer's service of

Morning Prayer, I'm praying with all who that morning are also praying it. And I'm praying prayers crafted not by my lonely piety, but by the church. I'm praying prayers that have their origin in another time and place—going all the way back to the early church—and thus I find myself mysteriously connected with believers that have gone before me.

Praying a daily liturgy, along with the weekly liturgy, helps me emerge from Markism. These prayers express more deeply what's going on in my soul because they connect me with the church's lived experience through the centuries.

Take for instance this prayer from Morning Prayer:

> Heavenly Father, in you we live and move and have our being: We humbly pray you so to guide and govern us by your Holy Spirit, that in all the cares and occupations of our life we may not forget you, but may remember that we are ever walking in your sight; through Jesus Christ our Lord. Amen.

When I look out at the "cares and occupations" that stretch before me in each morning, some of which discourage and some of which frighten me, I cannot think of anything better to pray.

Or this:

> Most merciful God,
> we confess that we have sinned against you
> in thought, word, and deed,
> by what we have done,

and by what we have left undone.
We have not loved you with our whole heart;
we have not loved our neighbors as ourselves.
We are truly sorry and we humbly repent.

There has been no better prayer that calls to mind the many ways I fail God, and at the same time covers the many sins I'm simply unaware of.

And on it goes. As I pray through Morning Prayer, time and again I find myself, even after years of praying, exclaiming, "That's exactly what I wanted to say!"

What I repeatedly discover in these prayers is not so much a poetic genius behind the words but a community in, with, and under the words. The first "community" is the Triune God, who empowers the liturgy with his presence. The second community is the church, which by the inspiration of the Spirit, has honed these prayers on the whetstones of history and suffering, with words shaped to a fine edge, prayers that express sharply the dull groans of the solitary soul.

Liturgy draws us then to the consummation of reality ("and blessed be his kingdom"). In the Bible, heaven is no ethereal existence—something less real. Instead, our current life is isolated and ghostlike compared with the thick physicality of the community to come, when we are joined to one another into deeper fellowship with the Triune God.

The liturgy pulls us into community, divine and human. Even when we pray these prayers alone in our closet, we are thrown into a fellowship of prayer that stretches back to the beginning, outward to the church, and forward to the kingdom. As we experience that story, we taste for a brief, stirring moment what it is like to be truly human again.

But the liturgy does more than lift us out of solitude. It calls us into a community of flesh and blood today. While the prayers *can* be said alone, they are designed to be said in a tangible fellowship of prayer. Like a compass pointing true north, they point us to the church. The prayers draw us together, like tributaries into a river, and now together as the church we rush back to the source.

But, as I noted above, I start to get uncomfortable at this point.

In the liturgy (especially the opening), says Orthodox theologian Alexander Schmemann, we declare the kingdom to be "the goal, the end of all our desires and interests, of our whole life, the supreme and ultimate value of all that exists." Then he adds, "The church is the assembly, the gathering of those to whom the ultimate destination of all life has been revealed and who have accepted it."

In other words, the liturgy comes packaged with the church. This package becomes a value meal; no substitutes allowed.

This is tough to swallow. The church has always been a worrisome and dysfunctional place where community-destroying sins—gossip, anger, envy, pride, among others—are fruitful and multiply. We rightfully expect much of those who publicly claim allegiance to the kingdom of God, and we are rightfully resentful when the church instead looks like a failed state.

No wonder many disciples bitterly abandon the church, striking out on their own, hoping against hope that, maybe as individuals shorn of religion, they can scale spiritual heights. Granite peaks do offer sweeping vistas, but they are lonely places. Saints like Francis of Assisi, Teresa of Avila, and Ignatius of Loyola, while knowing peak experiences, grounded themselves in the fellowship of prayer called the church. They knew that they could not ultimately love God whom they had not seen if they could not love those whom they could see.

When the liturgy places us squarely in the life of this community, it does so without illusions. Note the Roman Catholic liturgy's prayer of confession: "I confess to almighty God, and to you my brothers and sisters, that I have sinned through my own fault. . . ." before going to ask "my brothers and sisters, to pray for me to the Lord our God." This prayer assumes that worship takes place in a deeply flawed community—that the community constituted by the Trinity and destined for life in the kingdom is full of people who need to confess their sins and pray for one another.

The church is a community that together longs for healing, and is promised that it will receive what it longs for, not just as individuals but in union with others. Note the prayer as the church prepares to receive the Eucharist:

> Sanctify us also that we may faithfully receive this holy Sacrament, and serve you in unity, constancy, and peace; and at the last day bring us *with all your saints* into the joy of your eternal *kingdom*.

"They have been individuals, some white, some black, some poor, some rich," writes Schmemann. "And now they have been called to 'come together in one place,' to bring their lives, their 'world' with them and to be more than what they were: a new community with a new life."

St. Paul puts it this way: "So then you are no longer strangers and aliens, but you are fellow citizens with the saints and members of the household of God."

After praying the liturgy for a few years, it becomes impossible to pray alone, or to feel alone when we pray by ourselves. In the liturgy, we know instinctively that we are part of something bigger than ourselves and that something bigger is a community of love.

CHAPTER 4

THE INTIMATE OTHER

How the Liturgy Helps Us Meet a
Holy and Loving God

ONE REASON I WAS ATTRACTED TO BARB WAS HER APPARENT INTEREST IN THEOLOGY. We took religion classes together, we read German theologian Karl Barth together, and we co-wrote a paper on the Reformation. I was amazed to have discovered an eligible woman who shared this odd interest of mine. I proposed as quickly as I could.

Some weeks into the marriage, after I just finished some weighty tome—like Dietrich Bonhoeffer's *Creation and Fall*—I encouraged her to read it. She said she wasn't interested. Over the next few weeks, I suggested another theology book, and then another, only to be turned down repeatedly. I asked what was going on.

"I really don't like theology all that much."

"But what about . . . " I stammered.

"Oh, once in awhile it's okay. But most of the time I find it too dry."

I was floored. Here was the woman of my dreams telling me she wasn't the woman of my dreams.

As the years unfolded and we each matured in our own way, our differences became stark. She liked to rise early; I liked to stay up late—so when exactly were we supposed "to become one"? She remained a political liberal as I morphed into a conservative. She loved doing things on the spur of the moment; I planned spontaneity in advance. She was energized by a room full of people; the very thought of people drained me. She believed our kids should be given a break; I thought they should be more disciplined. We couldn't agree about where to vacation, what newspaper to subscribe to, or what color to paint the bathroom. We even had arguments about how to argue.

One day I stared at her across the kitchen table and wondered who this person was I was living with. A woman who had seemed to promise a lifetime of increasing intimacy turned out to be a stranger, an "other."

We don't enter a marriage to meet a stranger, and similarly, we don't enter a sanctuary to encounter an other. We come to church to connect with God. We've heard he is a loving heavenly Father, a friend, one who knows us, understands us, and identifies with our sorrows. He is the one who is closer than a brother. And so we come to meet him.

But when we walk into a liturgical service, we are confronted with a distant deity, who resides far away in heaven, a being of unimaginable power and authority, and who stands over and apart from us: "Glory to God in the highest," begins the Gloria. It continues:

> Lord God, heavenly King,
> almighty God and Father,
> we worship you, we give you thanks,
> we praise you for your glory.

Okay, we think, all well and good. So we hang on for a few minutes, hoping that soon the service will turn toward more spiritually intimate themes. But later, during the Creed—the summary of our faith—we hear the same sort of thing:

> We believe in one God,
> the Father, the Almighty,
> maker of heaven and earth,
> of all that is, seen and unseen.

Then it comes time to pray—finally, a chance for intimacy with our creator. And yet we find the liturgy's prayers are full of language about a God who seems unapproachable in his glory. Even the Lord's Prayer begins: "Our Father, *who art in heaven. . .* " As Karl Barth put it, "Heaven is part of the created world; that part of creation which is on high, unapproachable, incomprehensible."

Great. We've come to meet a Father God who loves us as children, but we find at key moments in the liturgy a God not near but high and lifted up—not like us but holy and mighty—not sharing in our weakness but full of power and might—not within us, but far away in heaven. God is worshipped as the Utterly Different One, as an Other. How are we to identify with, let alone feel comfortable with this sort of God?

Those of a philosophical bent may suspect that the liturgy's God is made in the likeness of the god of Platonic philosophers, those who are in love with abstraction and who revel in divine aseity (that God exists of and from himself). Nope. It's the God of the Bible that the liturgy helps us worship.

It is the God of the prophet Isaiah. Isaiah came to the temple one day and encountered not so much the God of Abraham,

Isaac, and Jacob—a God who had a personal relationship with his people, but instead he said he saw "the Lord sitting upon a throne, high and lifted up; and the train of his robe filled the temple." Some sort of angelic figures flanked the throne, but strange indeed was each of their appearance: "Each had six wings: with two he covered his face, and with two he covered his feet, and with two he flew." And if the complete Otherness of God had not been made plain, these strange spiritual beings were calling out, "Holy, holy, holy is the LORD of hosts; the whole earth is full of his glory!"

Isaiah was hardly alone. It seems that more times than not, when some biblical figure has a vision of God, it is alarming and incomprehensible. Ezekiel is another case in point. When he had a vision of God, he could not find the words to describe it. He too saw strange angelic figures, and "over their heads there was the likeness of a throne, in appearance like sapphire." Something like. In appearance like. He can't describe it.

The vision gets more confusing: "and seated above the likeness of a throne was a likeness with a human appearance." All well and good, but we're still trafficking in "seemed like." He continues: "Upward from what had the appearance of his waist I saw as it were gleaming metal, like the appearance of fire enclosed all around. And downward from what had the appearance of his waist I saw as it were the appearance of fire, and there was brightness around him." Ezekiel continues to struggle with language, and though in a valiant effort, he compares what he saw to a rainbow, in the end he just piles on the similes: "Such was the appearance of the likeness of the glory of the LORD." It wasn't *like* anything. It didn't *appear* as something. No—such was the *appearance of the likeness.*

Ezekiel is one confused prophet. Either that, or he met the true God.

The God of Isaiah and Ezekiel is the God of Jesus: Our Father, *who art in heaven, hallowed be thy name*—a God who always remains distant in some way, whose name, whose essence is sacred, holy, set apart from any reality we can comprehend.

The God of the Bible is the God of the liturgy. He is different, other. Fortunately, God is this and more.

My wife and I faced a choice when we saw each other as strangers. We could abandon one another and remain strangers. Or we could abandon our romantic illusions and become lovers.

For me, abandoning illusions meant recognizing the self-centered nature of the early intimacy I sought, in which I was infatuated with this woman because I was fascinated with me. I imagined she was a version of me with whom I could have guilt-free sex.

I had to accept the foreignness of my wife. She wasn't anything like me. She had emotions, interests, passions, prejudices, habits, politics, insights, weaknesses, and strengths all her own. I had to learn how to treat those differences not only with respect but with reverence. They made up this entity I called Barbara, a unique individual whom God had created and was fashioning as he saw fit.

If I was to truly become one with this other, it was this other with all her differences that I was going to have to become one with. Two can only become one if there are really two to begin with.

The same dynamic is at work in worship. Like most people, I'm desperate for intimacy with God, so my instinct is to glom onto prayers and songs that make God seem close. But when I begin here, I am tempted to identify God with the warm feelings such prayers and songs generate. I sing a "worshipful" song, and I get "worshipful" feelings—and I assume that's God. Do this habitually, thoughtlessly, prayerlessly, and it's easy to end up with a relationship with a glorified self.

But the liturgy puts a brake on narcissism right up front. When we are forcefully reminded that we are not worshiping an idealized form of the self, but a God "in heaven," a "holy" God, a genuine Other.

At that very moment, intimacy with God becomes possible. The possibility of mistaking God for the self has been taken off the table. Now a human self and the Divine Self—utterly unlike each other—begin to relate to each other. Union can come of these two.

We habitually point to the Incarnation as the event that signals the possibility of this union. Yes, but this ultimate miracle of intimacy has its own paradox.

"And the Word became flesh and dwelt among us," John says. Here the Gospel writer reminds us that the God of heaven became God on earth; the Holy One became one of us. We rightly see God's willingness to identify with us, to share our human lot. From this view, the Incarnation is God's reaching out to become intimate with us.

But in the Incarnation, God is also clarifying that he is a distinct Other, someone who exists apart from us and our spiritual feelings. In taking on bodily form, he made it impossible for us to believe that God is merely "the ground of being," "the universal or collective consciousness," "the higher self," or that he resides primarily in "the depths of the subconscious." In the objective, bodily presence of Jesus, we were reminded that God is not the same as our thoughts or feelings or religious experiences. The Incarnation is also testimony that God is not to be confused with us. He is an Other, and that means we can have a genuine relationship.

The Incarnation testifies to something else, as well. And this is the mystery of union with Christ: "I have been crucified with Christ," says Paul in one of his more mystical passages. "It is no longer I who live, but Christ who lives in me." Paul here describes the whole Christian life as union. Elsewhere he puts it more succinctly: "Christ in you, the hope of glory."

The liturgy is a place where this union with the Other is realized in extraordinary ways. The liturgy is infused with the presence of Christ from beginning to end, but the climax of intimacy comes when we partake of the body and blood of Jesus. It's one of those paradoxical moments when we know both the mystery of God's otherness and our union with him. The bread and wine are objects that have an existence and nature apart from us. We are human beings who are alive, active, and capable of enjoying relationships. Bread and wine are inanimate, inert, and mere things. And yet these foreign, impersonal substances become the means by which we are united with the most personal, active, and intimate of beings.

As one portion of the traditional Methodist eucharistic service puts it:

> Hear us, O merciful Father,
> we most humbly beseech thee;
> And bless and sanctify with thy Word and Holy Spirit
> these thy gifts of bread and wine,
> that we, receiving them
> according to thy Son our Savior Jesus Christ's holy
>   institution
> in remembrance of his passion, death, and resurrection,
> may be partakers of the divine nature through him.

Yes, "partakers of the divine nature." It doesn't get any more intimate than this. And it is the otherness of God that makes this union even possible.

This almost seems to be a law of intimacy: when we acknowledge and even celebrate the otherness of our lover, be it our spouse or God, we become partakers of their very life. My wife and I have over the years increasingly become partakers of one another. The two shall become one is not merely a physical and psychological reality of marriage. It is also an ontological reality—that is, our very beings mysteriously merge so that when one of us is off traveling, we each feel that some part of us is missing.

Life in Christ is both a partaking of his being, and a longing for his return. As much as we know intimacy with this Other, we also know that at this stage in history, something is missing. In the Holy Spirit, our lover is near—nearer to us than we are to ourselves. But he is far away in time, and we long for his coming again, when his dwelling place will be with us. So we know in this life both an indescribable intimacy and a powerful longing. As the liturgy says, from beginning to end,

> Blessed be God: Father, Son, and Holy Spirit.
> And blessed be his kingdom *now and forever.*

CHAPTER 5

IF YOU DON'T GET IT, YOU'VE GOT IT
The Liturgy as a Mystery Full of Meaning

"WE VALUE GOD-HONORING, UNDERSTANDABLE WORSHIP," announces one Pennsylvania church on its Web site.

A North Carolina church says, "Meaningful and understandable congregational participation in worship is essential."

If a church is trying to reach seekers, people who don't know Jesus and have had little acquaintance with church culture, it doesn't want them to feel lost and confused when they worship. The apostle Paul says as much when he cautioned the church in Corinth about excessive speaking in tongues: "For one who speaks in a tongue speaks not to men but to God; for no one understands him, but he utters mysteries in the Spirit."

So urging churches to avoid "speaking in the mysteries of the Spirit" is understandable and intelligible. But when it comes to the liturgy, this avoidance can become a problem: From beginning to end, the liturgy assaults us with one seeming absurdity after another—from the announcement of a coming blessed kingdom (what does *that* mean for those steeped in democracy?) to addressing a God who is three and yet one (how is that possible?) to talk of resurrection (seen anyone rise from the dead lately?)—and on it goes. The climax of the liturgy is a climax of non-sense:

The celebrant says, "The body of Christ, the bread of heaven"—but he's lifting up baked flour.

The celebrant says, "The blood of Christ, the cup of salvation"—but he's referring to fermented grape juice.

A Lutheran liturgy gathers a great deal of this non-sense together in this prayer:

> Remembering, therefore, his salutary command, his
>   life-giving passion and death
> his glorious resurrection and ascension, and the promise
>   of his coming again. . . .
> and with your Word and Holy Spirit to bless us, your
>   servants,
> and these your own gifts of bread and wine,
> so that we and all who share in the body and blood of
>   Christ
> may be filled with heavenly blessing and grace,
> and, receiving the forgiveness of sin,
> may be formed to live as your holy people
> and be given our inheritance with all your saints.

Life-giving death? Resurrection and ascension? Coming again? How can we "share" in the *body* and *blood* of another human being, let alone a man killed and buried two thousand years ago? And what's this talk of mortals being *filled* with *heavenly* blessings?

This is not exactly seeker-friendly.

Is it any wonder that churches that long to reach the unchurched—who hear *ascension* and *heavenly blessings* and *holy people* and think we're speaking in tongues—have run from liturgy?

Then in the midst of what seems like a cacophony of irrelevance comes a voice from long ago, speaking about God:

> To know him really is to know him as unknowable . . . God is something which in no sense is to be reached or grasped . . . God's worth and God's perfection cannot be put into words. When I say *man,* I have in my mind human nature. When I say *grey,* I have in my mind the greyness of grey. When I say *God,* I have in my mind neither God's majesty nor his perfection.

In this sermon, "The Divine Being," medieval mystic Meister Eckhart quotes Augustine, Bernard of Clairvaux, Gregory the Great, and the Bible to remind his listeners about a commonplace of Christian theology: God is incomprehensible.

A liturgical corollary of this truth is this: authentic worship of this God must, at some level, remain incomprehensible. Worship that enables us to encounter the living God should leave worshipers a bit stupefied; they should leave their pews, pump the minister's hand, and enthusiastically blurt out, "I didn't understand large portions of the service. Thank you."

This theological commonplace hints at a less seemly side of our natural desire for "understandable worship"—our desire for an understandable god, a god we can control. Just as we furiously pursue some line of study in order to "master" a subject, so we are tempted to pursue God in an attempt to master him. As A.W. Tozer put it,

Left to ourselves we tend immediately to reduce God to manageable terms. We want to get him where we can use him, or at least know where he is when we need him. We want a God we can in some measure control. We need the feeling of security that comes from knowing what God is like.

This is the problem of the moralist, who wants to box God into a set of religious rules, and of the rationalist, who imagines that God fits neatly into his systematic theology. This is also our problem when our longing for understandable and intelligible worship signals an unwillingness to love God as he is—ultimately mysterious and incomprehensible.

Worship that doesn't in some way leave a large space for transcendence and mystery is not fully worship of the God of the Bible, who when asked to name himself—to explain his essence—said rather truculently, "I am who I am."

The liturgy shines in the shadowy place called mystery. But to leave matters here, at the threshold of incomprehensibility, would also be leaving out something. For mystery is both more complicated and understandable than we imagine.

For those who saw the photo taken in May of 2006, it was an unremarkable picture of one baseball player shaking the hands of another from an opposing team. But for those who knew the story behind the handshake, that moment contained a world of meaning.

A few days earlier, A.J. Pierzynski of the Chicago White Sox had barreled over Michael Barrett of the cross-town rival, Cubs, in a close play at the plate. It was a "clean play" by baseball standards, but Barrett and Pierzynski still exchanged words, as competitive athletes are wont to do. Then Barrett threw a right hook that landed on Pierzynski's jaw, something professional baseball players are decidedly not supposed to do.

That led the batter in the on-deck circle to tackle Barrett, which led Cubs players to jump on both of them, trying to pull them apart. Both benches emptied and it was a free-for-all for about fifteen minutes before the umpires regained control of the situation. Four players were immediately ejected from the game, and punishments from the league office soon followed.

The handshake a few days later, then, was no mere handshake. The handshake conveyed a story—with characters, conflict, and reconciliation. And every time Pierzynski and Barrett shake hands in the years to come, they will in some sense re-live, re-present, that drama and that reconciliation.

The liturgy contains a similar "handshake" at its climax, an outward action that conveys a deeper drama. To some, this moment looks like routine ritual, like that handshake might have looked to those who had not heard what had happened a few days earlier. But those with eyes of faith see a mystery opening before them in the liturgy.

We call this moment in the liturgy a *sacrament,* an outward sign of an invisible reality. But it has also been traditionally called a *mystery,* though not because it is something that baffles us or eludes our understanding. Benedictine writer Jerry Driscoll puts it this way:

> The word *mystery* preserves the tension between the concrete and the divine. Something is definitely

present, but what is present exceeds and overflows the limits of the concrete, even if it is present only by means of it. This is mysterious, in a way unique to Christian understanding.

Like that handshake between two ballplayers, the sacrament conveys a deeper meaning. That liturgical handshake points to a fight and a reconciliation that entailed the crucifixion and resurrection of Jesus Christ. Every time we participate in this liturgical handshake, we relive in some sense that fight and reconciliation, that crucifixion and resurrection.

But here is where the analogy of the Barrett-Pierzynski handshake fails. That handshake merely recalls something that happened. The liturgical handshake—that is, the sharing of bread and wine at the climax of the service—not only recalls something that happened, but re-presents it in a way that makes it a present reality.

A minister says words and performs actions, but at a deeper level, it is Christ who is presiding. We share in bread and wine, but the reality is that we are taking Christ into us. It looks like this is all occurring in time and space, when in fact the boundaries of time and space are being shattered, when for a few moments "heaven and earth are full of [God's] glory."

When all is said and done, though it may look like we've done nothing more that re-enact a routine religious meal, in fact, as the concluding prayer notes, something terribly significant has occurred: "You have graciously accepted us as living members of your Son our Savior Jesus Christ, and you have fed us with spiritual food in the sacrament of his body and blood."

Or as the Lutheran prayer suggests, as a result of sharing the bread and wine, we will be filled with "heavenly blessing and grace," receive "the forgiveness of sins," "be formed" to live as a "holy people," and share in "our inheritance of all [God's] saints."

It sure doesn't look like any of this happened. Looks like we just ate bread and drank wine and said a few prayers. Looks like a handshake between two ball players. But the liturgy constantly reminds us that we have instead bumped into a divine reality. Keep doing this for a few years, and you'll soon be looking at the whole world differently.

First, you'll start looking differently at people in the pews around you. You'll start seeing that they are a holy mystery to be treated with as much reverence as you do the bread and wine. Benedictine Jerry Driscoll puts it this way:

> People just coming to the church building is already a mystery. A divine reality is hidden in their concrete coming. . . . Behind every one of the baptized who has come to celebrate Eucharist, stands a magnificent personal story of grace, of struggle, and labor and rejoicing, and of all these united around that person's faith.

Second, and as you step out the church doors and step through your week, you'll start to figure out that the world itself is a vast sacramental system, one cosmic mystery, a sign of something sacred and hidden. "The heavens declare the glory of God, and the sky above proclaims his handiwork," says the psalmist. "For his invisible attributes, namely, his eternal power and divine nature, have been clearly perceived, ever since the creation of the world, in the things that have been made," adds the apostle Paul.

After being discipled by the liturgy in this way, you will no longer be able neatly to divide the world into secular and sacred, material and spiritual, mystery and revelation. Every material thing will throb with the spiritual, and spiritual reality will be manifested in the material. And that may not always lead to a worship experience that is "understandable," but it will be more meaningful and relevant than worshipers can imagine.

CHAPTER 6

A MORE REAL CULTURE

*How the Liturgy Is More Relevant
Than We Can Imagine*

I WAS VISITING MY SON, who had recently moved to Denver, Colorado. I asked him if he had found a church home yet, and he said that he'd only visited two churches, one of which struck him as unusual.

On the one hand, it was full of twenty-somethings like himself. Very few older people or older families. "I've never been to a church with so many people my age," he said. He showed me the weekly bulletin, and the language and the graphics clearly said this was a church for twenty-somethings. The church was doing a lot of great things, from Bible studies to outreach to the homeless.

Then my son said, "I don't know how I feel about going to a church that caters to people my age. It seems like a church should be larger than one generation."

He was obviously attracted to the church, and yet felt some discomfort. He was feeling the discomfort of our age when it comes to church.

A recent book on "the missional church," argues that we need to "reinvent the church" in "revolutionary" ways so that we can "incarnate the gospel within a specific cultural context."

I found an example on the Internet recently—a church in Florida whose very name is Relevant.

Relevant is a casual, contemporary, Christian church meeting at the Italian Club in Ybor City, Florida. Our service is designed specifically for urban professionals and young families.

At Relevant, we feel that it's our responsibility to "clear the way" for you to come to church. We want you to be able to experience the great music, encouraging messages, friendly people and enjoyable atmosphere that are a part of Relevant.

This church, like the Denver church, is no doubt making a difference in the lives of urban professionals and young families precisely because it appears to be relevant.

Put the liturgical church in this context, and it's easy to see why liturgy can become a stumbling block. The worship leaders wear medieval robes and guide the congregation through a ritual that is anything but spontaneous; they lead music that is hundreds of years old; they say prayers that are scripted and formal. The "homily" is based on a 2,000-year-old book, and, the high point of the service is taken up with eating the flesh and drinking the blood of a Rabbi executed in Israel when it was under Roman occupation. It doesn't sound relevant at all.

But a closer look hints at something more profound going on. "The liturgy begins . . . as a real separation from the world," writes Orthodox theologian Alexander Schmemann. He continues by saying that in the attempt to "make Christianitity understandable to this mythical 'modern' man on the street," we have forgotten this necessary separation.

Precisely at this point the liturgy takes people out of their worlds and ushers them into a strange new world, to show them that, despite appearances, the last thing in the world they need is more of the world out of which they've come. The world the liturgy reveals does not seem relevant at first glance, but it turns out that the world it reveals is more real than the one we inhabit day by day.

The liturgy asks us to rethink what we mean by "relevant" worship.

For example, it is not an accident that when we think about making church more relevant, we usually have only one group in mind. In North America, that usually means twenty-somethings and young families. For one, twenty-somethings are some of the hardest people to attract to church, and two, only when they start raising families do they begin to return to church. It's a perfect target audience for a struggling or new church to strive to reach.

The discomfort my son couldn't articulate is that self-identified relevant churches, by their nature, limit a full-bodied expression of the church. In our worse moments, this approach appeals to immature motives. For example, I am currently in what many people consider a relevant and even "cool" church, and I have to admit I am proud of it. It's an interesting contrast to note how few churches that want to "reincarnate the gospel within a specific cultural context" want to do so among the poor, the homeless, welfare moms, drug-addicted men, or those trapped in nursing homes and convalescent hospitals.

This is one reason I thank God for the liturgy. The liturgy does not target any age or cultural sub-group. It does not even target this century (it does not assume, as we moderns are tempted to do, that this is the best of all possible ages, the most significant era of history). Instead, the liturgy presents a form of worship that transcends our time and place. Its earliest forms took shape in ancient Israel, and its subsequent development occurred in a variety of cultures and sub-cultures—Greco-Roman, North African, German, Frankish, Anglo-Saxon. The liturgy has been meaningfully prayed by bakers, housewives, tailors, teachers, philosophers, priests, monks, kings, and slaves. As such, it has not been shaped to meet any particular group's needs. It seeks only to enable people—people in general—to see God.

This may seem obvious—of course church is a place where we want people to see God. But we do get distracted. I was a pastor for ten years, an editor of a pastoral journal for four, and have been involved in leadership in my local church for eighteen years. I can't tell you the number of times I've argued that the church have "clear vision" or "passion for the lost" or "empowered laity" or "more spirituality" or "creative worship" and so on—all great things. How difficult it is to remember the fundamental need of our churches and the people who attend them: to see God.

Theologian and pastor Eugene Peterson talked about our desire for relevance in one interview: "I don't think people care a whole lot about what kind of music you have or how you shape the service. They want a place where God is taken seriously, where they're taken seriously."

The liturgy is indeed more relevant than we can imagine, because it takes God seriously, and therefore we are taken seriously. A liturgical service is by no means the only service that does this, but it is a form of worship that is especially suited to not getting distracted.

> Celebrant: Blessed be God: Father, Son, and Holy Spirit.
> People: And blessed be his kingdom, now and for ever.
> Deacon: Go in peace to love and serve the Lord.
> People: Thanks be to God.

The liturgy, from beginning to end is not so much about meeting our needs (though they will be addressed). The liturgy is about God. It's not even about God-as-the-fulfiller-of-our-need-for-spiritual-meaning. It's about God as he is in himself: Father, Son, and Holy Spirit. It is not about our blessedness but his. The liturgy immediately signals that our needs are not nearly as relevant as we imagine. There is something infinitely more worthy of our attention—something, someone who lies outside the self.

By constantly returning to *God* and *the kingdom,* the liturgy announces another order of reality into which we are being called. We are in the habit of thinking that our culture—the reality we strive to be relevant to—is the measure of meaning. That's why we're tempted to shape our churches to look like the culture, because that is what people in this culture will find meaningful. It is logical at one level, and there is no question that we have to be culturally sensitive in our outreach. But the liturgy wants to show us a deeper logic and relevance.

In third grade one day a few weeks into the school year, I was being corrected by my teacher, Mrs. Haller, for something I've long ago forgotten, but it was some minor infraction. What I do remember is that I started crying when she corrected me in front of the class. She was not being mean, but I was a very sensitive child, and I started crying because I had not pleased her.

Mrs. Haller then did something that surprised and matured me in the blink of a teary eye. First, she did not comfort me. I was waiting for her to do so, because obviously I had a need to be comforted. But Mrs. Haller took me more seriously than I was taking myself, even though I was taking myself very seriously, I thought. Second, she said very calmly and gently, "Mark, you're in third grade now. And we don't cry over matters like this anymore."

Immediately, I realized that none of my friends had cried over this sort of peccadillo since the school year started. I knew Mrs. Haller was right. She was calling me into a new reality in which expectations were different. She was calling me out of an old culture into a new one, in which boys and girls didn't cry when something small went wrong.

I wiped my face and returned to my seat, and I never did that sort of thing again. I was a third-grader now.

The liturgy begins by informing us that our culture needs not so much to be comforted as to gently and calmly be invited into an older and wiser culture—the culture of a Trinitarian God and his kingdom. This is what is blessed now and forever. Our culture is the transitory thing, an apparition that will someday have to pass away, just as childhood has to pass away. The liturgy greets us as we enter, "You're in the culture of God and his kingdom now. Things will be different from now on."

Before he became pope, Benedict XVI wrote, "The grandeur of the liturgy does not rest upon the fact that it offers an interesting entertainment, but in rendering tangible the Totally Other, whom we are not capable of summoning. He comes because he wills."

How exactly does God render himself tangible in the liturgy? In a number of ways, which we'll return to and explore further at various points in this book:

Certainly in the Eucharist itself, in which Jesus makes himself known in the breaking of the bread: "When he was at table with them, he took the bread and blessed and broke it and gave it to them. And their eyes were opened, and they recognized him."

Then there is the reading and preaching of the Word, the revelation of God to his people. This is not just a dramatic reading of an ancient and beautiful text, followed by an inspirational talk. God is speaking afresh to his people through the preached and spoken Word. As Jesus told the disciples before he sent them out to preach, and as he essentially tells every preacher: "The one who hears you hears me. . . ."

Less obviously, God makes himself known through the words and drama of the liturgy.

The words of the liturgy, as a quick glance will show, are Scripture-saturated, and thus carry a similar revelatory power as the formal reading of the lessons.

In addition, the very rhythm of the service—the liturgy of the Word followed by the liturgy of the sacrament, the praise that prepares us for the Word, the confessions and the prayers that guide our response to the Word—is a pattern that has been discovered rather than created by the church. This proved to be a holy pattern that within a couple of centuries began to seem "very meet, right, and our bounden duty" to practice in just this way.

As early as the second century the shape of the service took the form we use today. Let's look at one service in Rome as described by the church father Justin Martyr:

> And on the day called Sunday, all who live in cities or in the country gather together to one place, and the memoirs of the apostles or the writings of the prophets are read, as long as time permits; then, when the reader has ceased, the president verbally instructs, and exhorts to the imitation of these good things. Then we all rise together and pray, and, as we before said, when our prayer is ended, bread and wine and water are brought, and the president in like manner offers prayers and thanksgivings, according to his ability, and the people assent, saying Amen; and there is a distribution to each, and a participation of that over which thanks have been given.

One might assume that this was somehow especially relevant to Roman culture of that day, and in some ways it probably was. But what is interesting is that this liturgical shape became standard in the Western liturgy for the following centuries, which prompts us to wonder how this fits in the thousands of cultures the church encountered over the centuries. How in the world has it been relevant in the Middle East, North Africa, Europe, the Americas, and Asia? Yet it has been the basic outline in Catholic, Anglican, Lutheran, Presbyterian, and other communions, in so many cultures and eras.

Why this liturgy? Why this form? Because both its content and its shape have ushered people into a transcendent culture, where they meet the Trinitarian God and take their first baby steps in his kingdom.

In an old essay, F. H. Brabant put it this way: "All liturgical acts . . . have a double function: one directed Godward, expressing in outward form the thoughts and feelings of the worshipers, the other directed manwards, teaching worshipers how they ought to think and feel by setting before them the Church's standard of worship."

We have to pay attention to cultural context, no question. The history of liturgy has been in part about finding words and ritual that help people in a given culture to express their thoughts and feelings to God in ways that make sense. The liturgy has always had freedom and variety within its basic structure.

But it has steadfastly refused to let the culture determine its shape or meaning. Liturgical churches know that as profound a reality as is the surrounding culture, there is an even more profound reality waiting to be discovered. Like Mrs. Haller did for me, the liturgy gently and calmly gets us to open our eyes to the new reality, showing us the value of the "necessary separation" from the old. Suddenly, in the blink of an eye, we find our gaze directed away from ourselves and toward God and his kingdom. When we return to our homes, we are never the same.

CHAPTER 7

BIZARRE, HOLY MOMENTS
How the Liturgy Reshapes Our Sense of Time

THE MORE I GET TO KNOW OUR TWO DOGS, the more I realize how they naturally live by liturgical time.

The other morning, I was helping my wife load up supplies to take to a half-day retreat she was leading. As I stepped out the door with a load in each arm, Boomer, our one-and-a-half-year-old Australian Shepherd followed me. When I opened the trunk of my wife's station wagon, Boomer excitedly hopped in, turned toward me, and looked at me expectantly. I told him to get out, that we were not going to the park today. He sprang out and darted happily back into the house.

Boomer jumped in the car because he remembered the park. I don't know how dogs process the past, but he clearly had a sense of history at that moment.

He also had a sense of the future, in his own dog way. He anticipated that he would go to the park if he jumped in the car, and his eager face said as much.

When I told him to get out and get back in the house, he did it, assuming that whatever the Alpha-male in the house had in mind for the present, it must be good.

That's liturgical time in a nutshell, and it explains in part why this Anglican and this dog get along so well.

The beginning of the liturgy that re-orients our understanding of culture, also re-orients our sense of time:

Blessed be God: Father, Son, and Holy Spirit,
And blessed be his kingdom, now and forever!

If the service is about inviting us into a new world, it's also inviting us to enter a new time zone. This kingdom is a now-reality, which means it is a past reality made present and a future reality made present. It is thus a forever-reality.

The reality of God's in-breaking kingdom had a beginning. This mini-litany at the beginning of the liturgy harkens to the opening of Jesus' ministry when he announced, "the kingdom of God is at hand" (Mark 1:15). This liturgical beginning corresponds to a high point later in the service, when during the Eucharistic prayer, we say, "Christ has died, Christ is risen, Christ will come again." That is, Christ will come again to establish his kingdom.

In other words, the liturgy here and elsewhere joins past, present, and future in a mix that blurs time.

Take another example. Toward the beginning of the Eucharistic prayer, we break out in a praise we call the *Sanctus* (Latin for "holy"):

Holy, holy, holy, God of power and might.
Heaven and earth are full of your glory.

Though we sing this in the present, we recognize it as the prayer characteristic of God's people in the days of Isaiah the prophet:

Holy, holy, holy is the LORD of hosts;
the whole earth is full of his glory!

The *Sanctus* is also a prayer that characterizes eternity. As the seer of Revelation notes, all of heaven will eventually hymn:

Holy, holy, holy,
is the Lord God Almighty,
who was and is and is to come!

The liturgy so "confuses" time that it is difficult to tell what time it is when we sing this prayer during the service. There have been moments during the *Sanctus* when I have sensed that Isaiah and all the saints were at my side as we together praised God.

This shows that the liturgy is an experience of the kingdom in which past and future coincide in joyous present. Like Boomer, we are remembering a blessed past, anticipating a glorious future, looking expectantly now in the face of our Master.

The very day we gather for worship suggests this same melding of time. From the earliest days, the church recognized how the day of worship itself was playing with time. Sunday has three different designations: the first day, the day on which the Creator began his work—the third day as seen from the perspective of the cross—the eighth day, the culmination of the previous week and a sign of the kingdom to come. Thus the same day harkens to the key moment in salvation history (past), the daily rhythm of this present life (present), and that time when all things begin anew (future).

It is perfectly consistent, and hardly a superstition, to say that in each Eucharist Christ's sacrifice is made real once again. The Eucharist is not a re-sacrifice, a repeating of his death, but neither is it a mere mental recollection of a past event. The entire liturgy—with its radical sense of time—becomes a re-presenting of his once-for-all death and resurrection. It is made present to us. John the Baptist said it before the crucifixion, and we say it long afterward, but both of us say it as if it were happening before our very eyes: "Behold, the Lamb of God, who takes away the sin of the world!" (John 1:29).

In his role as *slaughtered* lamb, Christ *is* a life-giving presence *for eternity*. The futuristic Book of Revelation notes, "Then the angel showed me the river of the water of life, bright as crystal, flowing from the throne of God and of the Lamb through the middle of the street of the city."

The mention of water is not accidental. In Scripture, water has multiple and powerful connotations—from the waters at creation, to the flood of Noah, to the crossing of the Red Sea, to the baptism of Jesus. Water is a sign of both judgment and life, repentance and healing. We can hear in this passage from Revelation, echoes of John 9, the Pool of Siloam that heals, and of John 4, where Christ describes himself as "living water." This one little reference again joins past with future in a way that allows the present listener to wonder and rejoice.

This conflating of time is blessed because, among other reasons, the past is no longer a litany of failures to repress. The most significant event in my past is not a shameful transgression I can't forget but the death and resurrection of Jesus Christ. My past is not defined by my sin but by Christ's victory.

This new stance toward the past causes us to say the strangest things. Aleksandr Solzhenitsyn spent years in the brutal and dehumanizing Gulag of Soviet Russia. He writes in *The Gulag*

Archipelago that after his conversion to Christ, he began to notice how "slavery nurtures in you the shoots of contradictory feelings. . . . Formerly you never forgave anyone. You judged people without mercy. And you praised people with equal lack of moderation. Now an understanding mildness has become the basis of your uncategorical judgments. You have come to realize your own weaknesses—and you can therefore understand the weaknesses of others. . . . Your soul," he concluded, "which formerly was dry, now ripens from suffering."

Solzhenitsyn's sense of the past became so convoluted that he was able to write years later, "Bless you, Prison!" He looked at his past, which could have easily become nothing but a memory to repress. Instead, in Christ, it became a memory to bless.

Whether we've endured a history of sin or suffering, our past is not defined by our regrets but by Christ's redemptive work. The liturgy helps us see that Christ's death and resurrection were working their magic in, through, and in spite of our suffering and sin. We're nearly tempted to say, "Bless you Sin, for being in my life!"

Likewise, the future is no longer defined by the anxieties of our age. The future very well may include terrorism, disease, and environmental havoc; we may be called upon to suffer Alzheimer's disease or cancer. But this future does not define our Future, the ultimate reality toward which all of history moves. This is the Good News that transcends the daily news. Thus we live not by the predictions of experts and pundits, who make their living by the furrows of their brows, but by the sure and certain hope of Christ's coming.

The liturgy reminds us that the one thing truly needful has already been accomplished and is re-presented every time we participate in the Eucharist. Thus we are able to live in a kind of blissful present, in which the sorrows of the past and the anxieties of the future have been swallowed up.

Like Boomer, every present moment has the possibility of the park (the kingdom), where we've had so many good memories, and so many memories to come.

CHAPTER 8

WHAT YOU DON'T SEE IS WHAT YOU GET
How the Liturgy Changes Our Sense of Place

THE FIRST TIME I ATTENDED WORSHIP at my current church, I didn't feel comfortable. That's because the church worshiped in a school auditorium—in fact, the auditorium of the high school my children attended. I had been there for plays, music recitals, and award ceremonies. So to me, the auditorium smacked of mere high school. I couldn't get this notion out of my head as I worshiped that first Sunday.

I've now worshiped in this auditorium for three and a half years, so I've met God in this place over a hundred times. One evening recently, I sat in the same auditorium and listened to my high school daughter play in a concert. I kept thinking, *So what are these people doing messing with my worship space?* It felt odd watching a concert in a place I now associated with the worship of the Creator of music.

This sort of thing happens when we meet God in a place: that place becomes godly—holy, set apart in our hearts and minds.

In Scripture, we regularly see this dynamic at work. Take this example from the Book of Genesis: "God appeared to Jacob again, when he came from Paddan-aram, and blessed him. And God said to him. . . ."

Well, God said quite a few things. He gave Jacob a new name (Israel). He told him that "a nation and a company of nations shall come from you, and kings shall come from your own body." He promised him and his descendants the land he had given to Abraham and Isaac.

"Then," the writer of Genesis concludes prosaically, "God went up from him in the place where he had spoken with him."

Jacob is left astonished. Yet he does not consider this simply a "spiritual experience," something that occurred only in his heart and soul. This divine encounter took place—as all encounters with God take place—on a certain piece of real estate. Jacob also knew that he wasn't only a spiritual being, but also a physical being—a physical being who not only is required by his very existence to occupy one piece of real estate or another, but a physical being who is shaped by real estate. He does not pretend that where he lives and where he travels, let alone where he meets God, doesn't matter.

This place, the place where God met him, leaves a mark on Jacob, so Jacob leaves a mark on the place: As we read in Genesis: "And Jacob set up a pillar in the place where [God] had spoken with him, a pillar of stone. He poured out a drink offering on it and poured oil on it. So Jacob called the name of the place where God had spoken with him Bethel." The place he marked with a monument and a name became a place of worship. Both Jacob and this place had been changed by an encounter with God.

Sanctuaries are Bethel places, places where God meets and blesses his people. They are pieces of real estate where God leaves his mark on his people and on a place. Places become holy places, sacred spaces, places that people mark with stained glass or decorative altars or crucifixes. And they mark them by continuing to worship on this piece of real estate.

To be sure, we can worship God anywhere, and the church is not the building but the people. Yet this does not take into account how God normally works in our lives—that is, by revealing himself to us in places, places that become sacred and holy.

This is precisely why parishioners become feisty when someone wants to remodel the sanctuary in the least little way. And in the worst case scenerio, why they are distraught if a bishop decides to close their parish. And why they will fight to the death (or more precisely, to the debt) to keep their property out of the hands of their wayward denomination. This behavior, which is sometimes described as "worldly," is ultimately grounded in a biblical understanding of the world—that this planet contains spaces where God meets people.

Liturgical churches understand this reality. Thus their healthy addiction to magnificent worship spaces, whose very architecture evokes the reality of God's presence. But liturgical churches are also those that most likely (but not solely) idolize such places, treating them as if they have a holy existence apart from God. In some churches, it's as if the building has become the divine presence, as if the church *is* the building, as if this piece of real estate is a subdivision of the kingdom of heaven.

Those who pay close attention to the liturgy—those who refuse to mumble it as if they knew it all too well—will rarely make this mistake. They recognize not only the sacred nature of the place where they worship but that this place is not so easily defined and delimited.

The Academy Awards takes place in a particular place. Those who attend the Academy Awards—those inside in the hopes of receiving rewards and those outside hoping to get a glimpse of the stars—recognize that the Academy Awards is not limited by this place. As television cameras pan the crowds outside, for instance, then zero in on a particular person to ask his or her opinion of the latest arrival, that fan often smiles and waves at the camera, and then blurts out, "Hi, Mom."

Fans at the Academy Awards know that this is an event occurring in a space much larger than where they happen to be. They know that from across the world, people are looking in. Maybe even their moms.

The people of God at worship have this sense as well. Liturgical writer Jerry Driscoll puts it this way:

> For in the Eucharist the one time and place of a particular gathering—concretely existing in a specific culture and in a precise moment in history with all the life stories of those who have come together—are expanded and dilate and are made to contain in this particular form the mystery of the universal Church across the world and across the centuries and across the heavens extending to the community of saints and angels in heaven.

There are hints and allegations about this reality all through the liturgy. Take the invitation to the prayers of intercession in Lutheran worship: "With the whole people of God in Christ Jesus, let us pray for the church, those in need, and all of God's creation." This "whole people of God in Christ Jesus" cannot merely refer to those physically present on earth at that moment, but includes the "great cloud of witnesses" that the writer of Hebrews speaks of.

This reality is regularly affirmed whenever the church recites the Apostles' Creed: "We believe . . . in the communion of saints."

We are tempted to label such talk as "mystical," but it is more like liturgical common sense. This talk is based on a simple biblical premise: as we are one in Christ, so are those who have gone before us. If we are both one in Christ, then we are in union with one another, a union so strong and lasting that nothing can separate us, not even death. Certainly not time or space.

So while it may not be liturgically appropriate, it is certainly theologically sound to look up to heaven during worship, smile, and say (quietly), "Hi, Mom."

The liturgy messes with our sense of place in another way. Not only has the sanctuary become a much larger reality than we had imagined, it is not as fixed in place as we had thought. We can also conceive of the liturgy as a journey into the kingdom. It's as if in worship the entire sanctuary is lifted off its foundations to be transported to another place.

"Lift up your hearts," says the celebrant.

"We lift them up to the Lord," we respond at the beginning of the Eucharist. We are ascending, and ascending so quickly that within a minute or two the celebrant adds,

"And therefore we praise you, joining with the heavenly chorus, with prophets, apostles, and martyrs, and with all those in every generation who have looked to you in hope, to proclaim with them your glory, in their unending hymn."

Then the liturgy moves into a glorious hymn, as if the earthly church has now made its way into the heavenly realm:

Holy, holy, holy Lord, God of power and might,
Heaven and earth are full of your glory.

As we saw previously, this is a moment when past, present, and future have merged. The point here is similar: it is as if the places we call heaven and earth have merged, for as we approach the Eucharistic table, we have ascended into heaven. Or maybe it's that heaven has descended to earth. Or both, as the mystery suggests.

A worshiper at the Brotherhood of St. George, an Orthodox monastery in downtown Denver, approached one of the monks after a church service: "Father, did you get a chance to listen to those CDs I lent you?"

Father Christodoulos stood quiet for a few seconds. Then he said, "My mind is still on the liturgy. I haven't fully come back yet." Then he added, "The liturgy is heaven on earth. Paradise on earth. Maybe we shouldn't move beyond it so quickly to mundane things. Maybe we should take time to savor it."

The liturgy takes us to places we could not imagine, joining us with people and realities that defy the senses. Day by day, we live in a world that assumes that what you see is what you get, that you can't be in two places at the same time, that the "dead" are buried in cemeteries where bodies decay, and so on and so forth. The liturgy has always reminded the people of God that reality is so odd that here can be there and there can be here, that the dead are living and the living are dead. It harkens to a great mystery that our age cannot comprehend, that the people with whom we worship cannot be counted by a census taker, and that the place where we worship cannot be found on MapQuest—though it can be enjoyed even in a high school auditorium.

CHAPTER 9

LITTLE STILLNESSES
How the Liturgy Guides Us into Focused Grace

In *She's Got Next: A Story of Getting In, Staying Open, and Taking a Shot*, Melissa King writes about why she plays pick-up basketball:

> I've played because, when the game is good, when everyone is doing, not thinking, it happens, little stillnesses in the moments when you see your open man and nothing else, or you feel your shot going in the hoop as it leaves your hands, or you share a laugh with someone you've never spoken to.

John Brodie, quarterback of the San Francisco 49ers in my youth, described a similar experience: Sometimes during a game, he wrote,

> Time seems to slow way down, in an uncanny way, as if everything were moving in slow motion. It seems I have all the time in the world to watch the receivers run their patterns. . . . You can get into another order of reality, a reality that does not fit into grids and coordinates that most people lay across life.

That "order of reality" in sports is but a glimpse of a deeper order still, of course, one that Jesus says we can experience in the arena of life. He put it in the language of abiding:

> Abide in me, and I in you. . . . I am the vine; you are
> the branches. Whoever abides in me and I in him, he it
> is that bears much fruit, for apart from me you can do
> nothing. . . . If you abide in me, and my words abide
> in you, ask whatever you wish, and it will be done for
> you. (John 4–5, 7)

Little stillnesses. Another order of reality. Abiding in Christ. Prayer, and for our purposes, liturgy, is not something to be achieved. If we lay our "grids and coordinates" over it, we just get in the way of the gift that liturgy brings.

But getting in the way with our own grids and coordinates is what we do naturally.

I saw this happen on a recent retreat. Just before the speaker gave his talk, the song leader was supposed to lead us in a time of worship. So he directed us in singing a song that indeed focused our minds and hearts on Christ. Then he introduced himself, told a joke or two about his wife, got us chuckling. This liturgical rhythm was repeated twice more before the speaker finally stood before us. The song leader was laying his grid—entertainment—over the worship, and as a result, I had a difficult time trying to worship Christ.

Of course, I don't need the help of an enthusiastic worship leader; sometimes I lay my own grids and coordinates over worship. Some Sundays, I am desperate to have a "meaningful" worship experience; so I valiantly try to put myself in a spiritual mood as I enter the sanctuary. I say all the prayers with inward fervor. I confess my sins with profound sincerity. I listen attentively to the sermon. I receive the Eucharist with great reverence.

And I walk out of the sanctuary irritated.

It's obvious why I haven't had a "meaningful spiritual experience." I spent my time focusing on the experience I was supposed to be having rather than on the Lord I was supposed to be worshiping. That's laying a grid; that's getting in the way.

We have been raised in an achievement culture, a culture in which aphorisms like "Nothing can stop the man with the right mental attitude from achieving his goal" (Thomas Jefferson) and "The value of achievement lies in the achieving" (Albert Einstein) are imprinted on our genes from birth. There are many arenas of life in which striving and straining make for success. But worship is not one of them.

Instead, in the liturgy, we are invited to enter another order of reality: "Blessed be his kingdom, now and forever!" This is not something we can achieve as much as simply abide in.

"To wait patiently for." "To remain in a place." "To dwell." Such are some of the definitions of *abide*.

The word that Jesus uses in John is the same word Luke uses in Acts when he wrote, "[They] went on ahead and were waiting for us at Troas" (Acts 20:5). Paul's friends in Troas could do nothing to hurry or force Paul's arrival. If they tried too hard, they might mess things up. They could miss Paul's arrival by going out to meet him, especially if they guessed wrong about his travel plans. If they simply gave up, and left the house where they were staying, they might also miss him. They were required to do something that was both hard and easy. Hard because it required them to wait in a certain place and to do so patiently. But easy: that's all that was asked of them—to wait.

The liturgy is the place where we wait for Jesus to show up. We don't have to do much. The liturgy is not an act of will. It is not a series of activities designed to attain a spiritual mental state. We do not have to apply will pressure. To be sure, like basketball or football, it is something that requires a lot of practice—its rhythms do not come naturally except to those who have been rehearsing them for years. On some Sundays the soul will indeed battle to even pay attention. In the normal course of worship, we do not have to conjure up feelings or a devotional mood; we are not required to perform the liturgy flawlessly. Such anxious effort only lays grids and coordinates over the liturgy that blind us to what is really going on.

We do have to show up, and we cannot leave early. But if we will dwell there, remain in place, wait patiently, Jesus will show up.

He shows up in the reading of Scripture, the Word. It is no coincidence that both Jesus and the Scriptures are called the Word of God. Theologians debate the exact relationship between the two, but most traditions meld their authority. Many services include this response at the end of the readings:

Reader: The Word of the Lord.
Congregation: Thanks be to God.

When the Gospel is read, the whole congregation stands, as if Jesus has just walked into the room. We recognize that the very words of Christ are about to be read; the very actions of Christ about to be unveiled. We lean forward, and turn an ear, anxious to miss nothing. It's as if we are hearing and seeing Jesus again.

In fact, we are, as the congregation's response is so personal.

Before the Gospel is read, these words are spoken:

> Reader: The Holy Gospel of our Lord Jesus Christ,
>   according to [John or another Gospel]
> Congregation: Glory to *you*, O Christ.
> And after:
> Reader: The Gospel of the Lord.
> Congregation: Praise to *you*, Lord Christ.

Jesus also shows up in the preaching. "The one who hears you hears me," Jesus told his disciples as he sent them out (Luke 10:16a). And preachers since have understood that in one sense the preaching about the Word of God is the Word of God. It is not the revealed Word of Scripture, but it is a chief way by which Christ continues to speak to us.

What Richard John Neuhaus wrote about "great" preaching applies to all preaching: "It is an Emmaus-like experience in which the Scriptures are opened up and you recognize Christ, and with him, with a fresh sense of discovery, you see the truth about yourself and your world."

For years I served a preacher who struggled in this part of his pastoral calling. As he himself admitted, his homiletic structure was often incoherent. He struggled to find engaging illustrations. But in every sermon there appeared at least one sentence that startled me with the fresh sense of discovery and a fresh vision of Jesus.

Naturally, as noted elsewhere in this book, Jesus also shows up in the Eucharist. To receive the bread and wine is to receive

Christ: "Whoever feeds on my flesh and drinks my blood," he said, "abides in me, and I in him." The celebrant simply asserts this miracle when he offers the bread and wine:

> The body of Christ, the bread of heaven.
> The blood of Christ, the cup of salvation.

Listening to the written and spoken word, opening one's hands to receive the bread and one's mouth to receive the wine—these are not achievements. Indeed, they mostly require abiding—staying in place, looking for the arrival of God.

These two movements of the service—Word and sacrament—are not just momentary climaxes but also signs of Christ's presence throughout the service. "Where two or three are gathered in my name," Jesus says, "there am I among them." When we worship with the body of Christ, we are *in* the body of Christ, not just as a metaphor, but as a spiritual reality: we in Christ, Christ in us.

Lutheran theologian Anders Nygren wrote, "The Church is Christ as he is present among us and meets us upon the earth after his resurrection. . . . Christ is present in his Church through his Word and Sacrament, and the Church is, in its essence, nothing other than the presence of Christ."

Nygren expresses theologically what the service does liturgically: it allows us to know the presence of God and hear the still, small voice—one of those little stillnesses, when we enter another order of reality.

CHAPTER 10

WE WORSHIP A MATERIAL SAVIOR
Why the Liturgy Engages the Whole Body

I T'S HARD TO TELL WHETHER WE LOVE OR HATE OUR BODIES. On the one hand, note the loving attention we pay them. We dress them, pierce them, color them, tattoo them, and decorate them with jewels. We show off our busts with low-cut dresses and our rippling biceps with sleeveless shirts. We've created entire industries—dieting and exercise—to ensure that our bodies stay fit.

So we must love our bodies.

Then again, all this attention might signal how much we hate our bodies. Perhaps it's all a vain attempt to distract others from seeing our less graceful features. We've created the fitness industry precisely because we're *not* fit. Our bodies never seem to be in the right shape. Our breasts are too small, our hips too large, and our muscles too flabby. We don't feel fit for public consumption.

Those who struggle with "sins of the flesh"—gluttony and lust, to name two of the more popular varieties—would certainly agree. This phrase, however antiquated, seems all too apropos to those who war daily with fleshly desires. Like Paul, they know they are losing and cry out, "Who will deliver me from this body of death?"

So the body seems to be the enemy, and for some, Christianity is a way to transcend the body. Though not many today follow in the footsteps of Francis of Assisi, who called his body "Brother Ass" and sought to tame it with ascetic disciplines, many of us would love to conquer the "weakness of the flesh."

No wonder that many find liturgical services troubling. The liturgy seems, well, so worldly. Just when we're trying to transcend the body, the liturgy keeps pointing us back to it. Here we find religion that traffics in the body, that even celebrates the flesh.

Let's begin with a reminder of how much the Scripture integrates body and worship:

> Oh come, let us worship and *bow down*;
> let us *kneel* before the LORD, our Maker!
> —Psalm 95:6

> I desire then that in every place the men should pray,
> *lifting holy hands.* . . .
>   —1 Timothy 2:8

> Hear the voice of my pleas for mercy,
> when I cry to you for help,
> when I *lift up my hands*
> toward your most holy sanctuary.
> —Psalm 28:2

> At the name of Jesus *every knee should bow*, in heaven
> and on earth and under the earth, and *every tongue confess*
> that Jesus Christ is Lord.
> —Philippians 2:10–11

Likewise, the appreciation of the body is woven throughout the liturgy. Take, for example, how the Nicene Creed talks about Jesus Christ:

> by the power of the Holy Spirit
> he became incarnate from the Virgin Mary,
> and was made man.
> For our sake he was crucified under Pontius Pilate;
> he suffered death and was buried.

The Eucharistic prayer says the same thing more succinctly: Jesus came "to share our human nature, to live and die as one of us."

The liturgy does not point us to "the Christ spirit," "the ground of all being," "the Universe," or any other amorphous, abstract spiritual entity. Instead it points us to the one who did not think Pure Spirit a thing to be grasped. He who created flesh and called it very good, put his money where his divine mouth was, and took on bodily life and lived among the embodied. To put it simply: we worship a material Savior.

We cannot worship a material Savior without the material. So how do we worship the one who made himself like us in every respect? We make our worship to be like him in every respect: We traffic in the bodily senses, the five organs through which reality comes to those who dwell in flesh and blood: We observe the symbols of the faith; we hear the Word; we smell the prayers of incense; we touch and taste the sacramental life.

This is the way bodily creatures love one another. When husband and wife know they will make love in the evening, they prepare themselves: by dressing attractively, dabbing on perfume and cologne, speaking romantic words, caressing one another—all the senses are put to good use. The creator of our bodies loves us no less, and wishes to engage us with every sense.

Though Jesus comes to us through the Spirit, he does so in the material. Since the Incarnation, there seems to be no other way.

We grasp this paradoxical reality in many spheres. I drive through my old neighborhood, by the home I spent my teenage years, and I am flooded with immaterial emotions and thoughts and am left nostalgic for hours. I get a whiff of an apple pie, and I am ready for dessert. One friend gives me a handshake, another a hug, and my wife something more, and each physical expression conveys different shades of love and intimacy.

How much more when it comes to Jesus. When we visit a prisoner or give drink to the thirsty or put clothes on the naked, he says, we have met him spiritually and physically.

As the Episcopal Book of Common Prayer notes, in "the water of Baptism . . . we are buried with Christ in his death. By it we share in his resurrection. Through it we are reborn by the Holy Spirit."

And as the bread is offered to us, the celebrant says, "The Body of Christ, the bread of heaven" and when the cup is offered, we are told, "The Blood of Christ, the cup of salvation."

These are visible, material signs that lead us to things invisible and spiritual.

And yet we balk, especially the more Protestant among us. Our long distrust of idolatry—when the material moves from means to end—has often wrecked havoc. We've seen churches that spend inordinate energy ensuring that their material worship is done decently and in order, all the while ignoring

God. This is not a new problem, as the prophets, speaking in the name of Yahweh, were keen to point out:

Bring no more vain offerings;
     incense is an abomination to me.
New moon and Sabbath and the calling of
     convocations—
I cannot endure iniquity and solemn assembly.
Your new moons and your appointed feasts
     my soul hates;
they have become a burden to me.

But God never asks us to abandon material worship, as if that were possible. Even when we strip down the service to its barest essentials—the Word read and preached—we find ourselves tied to the material: After all, it is through vocal chords and sound waves and ear drums, and through light rays and paper and ink that the Word comes to us.

So the question instead is how to use the material to worship aright. The caution of idolatry is not intended to get us to abandon material worship, but to test it. Does our material worship lead to narcissism—a preoccupation with our pomp and rituals (it's so beautiful or uplifting or even heavenly)? Or does it lead us into the presence of Almighty God, who greets us in love and then sends us into the material world "to do justice and love kindness."

That's one large reason both the Bible and liturgical traditions focus so much on the body. Bodily worship prepares us with bodily exercises, so to speak, to get us into shape to serve the world.

One liturgical theologian put it this way:

> This is why the [L]iturgy not only expresses what we feel; it also teaches us what we ought to feel. The genuflection, even if it is done with little conscious devotion, stands for an ideal of adoration, and often the very act itself awakens our sluggish attention.

Similarly, raising hands in praise helps me feel praiseful, passing the peace with handshakes and hugs connects me to other human beings, and standing for the Gospel reading engenders reverence. All the actions of the liturgy subtly and profoundly shape our character so that we go forth into the world better able to love and serve.

More than anything, of course, we are able to carry the love of Jesus into the world because we've been touched by him in worship. According to one desert father, Abba Apollo, who lived in the fourth century, the devil has no knees. Therefore he cannot kneel or adore or pray. One Catholic bishop comments,

> Being unwilling to bend the knee at the name of Jesus is the essence of evil. But when we kneel at Jesus' name, when we bow down in service of others, and when we bend the knee in adoration, we are following in the footsteps of the Magi, we are imitating Blessed Mother Teresa of Calcutta, Saint Maximilian Kolbe, and all the saints and angels in heaven.

And that completes the circle. In worship, we meet Jesus in the bread and wine. In service, we meet Jesus in the prisoner, the sick, and hungry. In this material life, we cannot escape the material Savior, who does not leave us or forsake us, whether we're in church or in the world.

CHAPTER 11

LEARNING BY LAUGHING
How the Liturgy Teaches Us the Faith

I WAS BAPTIZED INTO PHYSICS IN FIRST GRADE. That's when I learned Newton's three laws of motion: the law of inertia, the law of acceleration, and the law of reciprocal actions. That is:

1. An object in motion will remain in motion unless acted upon by a force.
2. Force equals mass multiplied by acceleration.
3. To every action there is an equal and opposite reaction.

I also learned what an axis of rotation is, and that $F = ma$ (the force on an object is equal to its mass multiplied by its acceleration). I didn't learn this formula, however, just its reality.

None of this took place in a formal classroom, but on the classroom we call the playground. Specifically I was schooled in physics on the merry-go-round, where all of Newton's laws of physics were felt deep within the body.

On that merry-go-round my friends and I learned other things. Like courage ("I dare you to . . . .") and wisdom (i.e., you should not try to jump on a merry-go-round if it is spinning fast). But in particular I learned about joy as we pushed the merry-go-round to what seemed to us incredible speeds, as the wind blew in our faces and our bodies bent outward by some magical force, and we held on for dear life, laughing.

As I remember it, it makes me think of the Christian education we receive on the merry-go-round we call liturgy.

We are in the habit of thinking of Christian education taking place in a classroom on Sunday mornings before or after worship—Sunday school. We might add small group Bible studies, the occasional Saturday seminars, weekend retreats, and morning devotions. That's more or less the education part of the Christian life for most of us.

But as important as these elements are, they do not get at the heart of *Christian* education, nor the heart of Christian *education.*

Sunday school and small groups shape us in important ways. The classroom is a great setting to learn the content of Bible stories. The living room is an ideal place to wrestle collectively with a passage of Scripture or a book on spiritual direction. But these settings are recent innovations—Sunday school in the 1780s, and small groups in the 1960s. Long before these experiments came into being, the church had found another setting where theological education of the most profound sort was offered. To understand how the liturgy educates us theologically first requires a little history.

In the West, education today normally takes place within a classroom, where a teacher transfers content to pupils. Knowledge is usually considered a repository of neutral facts conveyed by an expert in teaching, and the mastery of these facts is the goal of education.

This is sometimes called an "objectivist" view of learning, and while it is being challenged in many quarters, it is still deeply embedded in our culture. It is part and parcel of the larger quest for an "objective truth" pursued by the autonomous, free individuals, without the constraints of any authority—that is, tradition, history, and community.

"Christian education" has been practiced in this way for the last couple centuries. It has followed a model emphasizing classroom instruction and curriculum development, as well as depending on an expert teacher. The approach is favored by traditions that place the pulpit at the center of worship, giving priority to the teaching of the Word.

This educational approach has done some wonderful things. It is an efficient way to impart Bible facts, a Christian worldview, and an explanation of the core doctrines of the faith. Who does not relish sitting at the feet of a gifted teacher or preacher?

But the "educational system" of Jesus was rooted in a different approach: living in and with a community. Not only was theology imparted by a teacher, but it was also *lived together* in the context of community prayer. This system is not as interested in scientific and unbiased knowledge as it is in subjective knowledge—that is, it wants to create an "irrational" loyalty to Jesus and an over-the-top concern for others.

This is why Paul, when he prays that his congregations might grow in *knowledge,* is clearly referring to something that transcends mere intellectual cognition: In his prayer for the Ephesians, he asks

> that the God of our Lord Jesus Christ, the Father of glory, may give you a spirit of wisdom and of revelation in the knowledge of him, having the eyes of your hearts enlightened, that you may know what is the

hope to which he has called you, what are the riches of his glorious inheritance in the saints, and what is the immeasurable greatness of his power toward us who believe.

This knowledge is not just about doctrine, but about apprehending a new reality ("having the eyes of your hearts enlightened"), as well as experiencing hope, power, and grace. Not only is it is a prayer for a community, but one that can only be fulfilled in community—"toward *us* who believe."

One way to participate in this communal educational experience is to participate in liturgy. Here the education imparted is not primarily about grasping ideas—though it does include that. It is knowledge that comes by participation in the community of God.

Again, note how at the beginning the liturgy highlights the new community we are participating in: "and blessed be his kingdom, now and forever." But we *experience* that communal education at various points in the service, not just with our minds, but with our very bodies. For example, when we pass the peace, we say to one another:

"The peace of the Lord be with you."
"And also with you."

This ritual act is not intended merely to "remind" us that members of the church should be reconciled to one another before they take the Eucharist. No, the act itself—of turning to others, of shaking hands or embracing, of looking each other in the eye, of speaking peace to one another—is to step onto the merry-go-round of community. And it can make you dizzy or nauseous or joyous depending on who you are making peace with.

Let us consider the Eucharist. We are not just watching an audio-visual presentation of the death and Resurrection of Christ. There are better, more affective ways of re-creating, emotionally and visually, those events of long ago. Instead, as we participate in the Eucharist, we participate in the death and Resurrection of Christ as it is being re-presented. Not repeated, but presented afresh, destroying the boundaries of time and space for a moment.

As we partake of bread and wine we are not just reminded of Christ's body and blood, and therefore reminded of his bodily death on a cross, and thus reminded of the doctrine of the atonement. There is that—but so much more. We are taking into ourselves the crucified Savior. We are participating in the power of his resurrection. We're not just thinking about that power, but standing on the merry-go-round of resurrection power, spinning faster and faster.

Granted, we do not always enjoy a primal sensation when doing the liturgy. That is due in part to our retreat from a world of connectedness and our having been discipled in a world of objectivity. We have gotten so used to divorcing mind from body—and spirit from both—that we hardly know how to learn bodily any more. In addition, spiritual sensations are more subtle and mysterious than we imagine. The spiritual palate must be trained to taste the sweetness of the holiness of the bread and wine.

Sometimes the liturgy doesn't affect us emotionally because of the mysterious workings of the Spirit: The Holy God refuses to be manipulated even by liturgy, and sometimes withdraws all sensible evidence of his presence so that we will walk by faith, not by sight or feeling. The fact that liturgy can become routine, so routine that we don't even notice what is happening to us, doesn't take away from the reality of the bodily education that is going on—any more than the routine of dinner with family takes away from what it teaches us about love.

To be sure, there is objective education in worship. A careful study of the liturgy will teach us much about the Trinity, the Incarnation, and the other core doctrines. But the liturgy is not primarily about doctrinal education any more than family dinners are primarily about nutrition. Worship is not a creative Sunday school class.

Robert Webber and Rodney Clapp note our temptation to justify worship on all sorts of pragmatic grounds. But worship is

> first and finally the service of God and needs no other justification. The transformation of worshipers is not its central aim. In fact, we are not apt to be changed by worship if we come to it primarily to be changed, for then we will be back to concentrating on ourselves. The transformation of the church is a by-product of the liturgy. It occurs only when the church is determined foremost to simply worship God.

In the life of faith, we certainly need classrooms and curriculum. There is, after all, that pesky commandment about loving God with the mind. But we don't enter worship to learn *about* God any more than I stepped on a merry-go-round to learn Newton's laws of motion. Something more much mysterious is going on in both.

Liturgical theologian Aidan Kavanaugh sums it up well: "The liturgy, like the feast, exists not to educate but to seduce people into participating in common activity of the highest order, where one is freed to learn things which cannot be taught"—spinning round and round, hanging on for dear life, and laughing.

CHAPTER 12

LIVING IN THE TRINITY
How the Liturgy Changes Us
at the Very Core of Our Being

To be honest, I do not want to love God perfectly. I like to love him sometimes, but I need a break from God now and then. Even when I feel like loving him, I always hold something back. I'm frightened of loving God perfectly. I don't know what he'd want of me, and I'm too scared to even think about it. I live a pretty good life, and most people would consider me pretty religious. But it's respectable religion I enjoy; religion that leaves me some personal space.

I've spent a lot of energy in my life making sure I have some space. I've never loved anyone or anything whole hog. I've always held something back, lest I get hurt, lest I start feeling trapped, lest I find myself having to do things I really don't want to do. It's one reason I've battled loneliness my whole life. But given that I keep up this pattern, I must think the trade off worth it.

In contrast to this lifestyle, I find this unnerving prayer at the beginning of the liturgy I participate in every week:

Almighty God, to you all hearts are open, all desires known, and from you no secrets are hid: Cleanse the thoughts of our hearts by the inspiration of your Holy Spirit, *that we may perfectly love you,* and worthily magnify your holy Name; through Christ our Lord. *Amen.*

That we may perfectly love God—yikes! But that is what the liturgy intends to do to us, help us perfectly love God. And it's the reason I keep participating in liturgical worship. A person like me needs to be reminded regularly that I have been made for this. And I need practice at this love. When it comes to love, the liturgy is both teacher and coach.

The liturgy reminds me that I've been made to love God "perfectly." It doesn't mean perfect in some abstract ethical sense, love with no mistakes. A perfect evening with a lover doesn't mean every course of the meal was delicious or that every part of the conversation sang. It means that the evening as a whole contained all the elements that go into a romantic evening: good food and wine, engaging conversation, and a slow and elegant dance toward union. As my wife and I lie in bed afterward thinking about the shape of the whole evening, including that brief argument before dessert, we're still apt to say, "That was a perfect evening." To love God perfectly means to love God fully, with heart, soul, mind, and strength. We've noted in various ways how the liturgy engages heart, soul, mind, and strength, but we've only skimmed the edges when it comes to the Object of love. The liturgy does not hesitate to repeat the essential nature of that Object, and it does so because once we know and experience this particular God, loving him perfectly becomes that much more possible.

The God of the liturgy is a Trinity, from beginning ("Blessed be God: Father, Son, and Holy Spirit") to end ("The blessing of God Almighty, Father, Son, and Holy Spirit").

When we think of the Trinity we tend to think of the *doctrine* of the Trinity. A doctrine is not an easy thing to love; most of us cannot love theological terms and formulas. Indeed, it is crucial to understand that Jesus' relation to the father is *homoousios* (Greek: of *the same* essence) and not *homoiousios* (Greek: of *similar* essence). There is a certain elegance and symmetry to the Nicene Creed's phrasing: Jesus is described as "God from God, light from light, true God from true God. . ."and so forth. Elegance and symmetry are things one can admire, not necessarily love.

Yet what is hidden in, with, and under the theology is an understanding of the Trinity that will transform us. It is this understanding that the liturgy traffics in, because it is grounded in Scripture, and when Scripture talks about God, the language gets very personal. Note how Jesus talked about his relationship to the Father—this from a prayer for his disciples:

> The glory that you have given me I have given to them, that they may be one even as we are one, I in them and you in me, that they may become perfectly one, so that the world may know that you sent me and loved them even as you loved me. . . . I made known to them your name, and I will continue to make it known, that the love with which you have loved me may be in them, and I in them."

This prayer comes at the culmination of chapters 14–17 in John's Gospel, chapters in which Jesus mentions the various ways he is one with the Father and the Spirit:

- If you had known me, you would have known my Father also.
- Whoever has seen me has seen the Father.
- I am in the Father and the Father is in me.
- When the Spirit of truth comes . . . he will not speak on his own authority, but whatever he hears he will speak, and he will declare to you the things that are to come. He will glorify me, for he will take what is mine and declare it to you.

From these and other New Testament passages, we see that the unity of the Trinity is not merely formal and logical; it is also a unity of purpose. Most importantly, it is a unity of love. More importantly still, while most biblical passages about God's love emphasize God's love toward us, in John 17, the veil separating us from God is lifted briefly, and we see that God's love exists apart from his love for us.

Upon this revelation the heart of Christian faith and life rests. If we get this—that God's love exists apart from his love for us—we understand the meaning of human existence.

One consequence of this revelation is this: God's love for us is not based on his need for love and fellowship—as if we were necessary for a God of love to be complete, as if God *needed* us. This cannot be true of the Trinitarian God. This God has known perfect love from before the creation of time and space. He created us not because he had to have someone to love to be self-fulfilled as God, but because the love of the Father, Son, and Holy Spirit bubbled over into creation.

Given the type of love with which we reciprocate—something less than perfect love—this is a remarkable grace. God is slumming when he loves us. He doesn't need our paltry love, and yet he reaches out to us in love, wanting us to grab his hand in love, simply because, well, he wants to.

A second crucial part of this revelation is this: This Trinity-in-love, this Loving Trinity whom the liturgy worships, is the God in whose image we have been created. If loving communion is at the core of the Trinity, it is at the core of who we are.

Since the Enlightenment, we in the West have thought of ourselves more as solitary individuals, and individuals mostly defined by mind, by intellect. As Descartes put it, "I think, therefore I am."

While this insight has blessed the Western world in many ways, it has led to an excruciating loneliness, as well, which the nineteenth- and twentieth-century existentialists (Camus, Sartre, among others) articulated so powerfully, and in the twenty-first century, has led to a deep despair, as expressed by many postmodern philosophers. When the individual is our starting point, we can find no way to satisfy the basic yearning of the human heart, which has been created for communion.

My instinctive starting point with others and with God is that I am the solitary individual who, as I feel like it, will reach out to others—but I always reserve the right to withdraw back into my cocoon. I think, therefore I am, and everything else is frosting.

The biblical, liturgical, Trinitarian starting point, by contrast, says, "I love, therefore you are. You love, and therefore I am." Our existence begins not with the solitary individual ruminating alone about the core of human identity, but with the creation of two people in the image of the Trinitarian God, who exists eternally in relationship: "So God created man in his own image, in the image of God he created him; male and female he created them" (Genesis 1:27).

The question "Who am I?" cannot be answered without answering the question "Who are *we*?" We cannot conceive of ourselves (without stumbling into mere abstraction or without doing violence to who we are) until we conceive of the other—any more than we can conceive of one person of the Trinity without at the same time conceiving of the other persons. At a very practical level, no human life can survive without the reciprocation of love.

This profoundly communitarian ethos is woven all through the liturgy because the liturgy is profoundly Trinitarian. If we pray it often enough, it will begin to radically shape our lives. We'll start to discover that our primary duty in life is not to find ourselves, not to develop our gifts, nor to make sense of life. Instead we'll realize that we are called to love others so that they can come into existence, while they do the same for us.

This includes the miracle of creating babies, but it also means bringing already breathing beings into true existence. A simple example: as a teenager, my church youth director told me he wanted me to prepare a devotional for one of the weekly meetings. I objected, saying that I was not ready or capable of doing so. He said I was being silly, that I was indeed ready, and insisted I prepare the devotional. I've had many such encounters in my life, when people have seen something in me that I have not seen in myself, and they have called it forth out of the chaos. They have created me, made me who I am today.

Sharing a meal or conversation, or even sitting in silence with another, is an act that validates the existence of the other. Even we introverts recognize that life would be unbearable—I mean this literally, that is, I would likely commit suicide—if we didn't have people in our lives. People like me may find it difficult to create or sustain intimacy, but because that intimacy is available to entice (and frighten) me, my life is not only bearable but possible.

This all starts when we are first loved by a communitarian God into a communitarian existence. And thus we share in the mission of this Trinity, which is to create and sustain other beings in love.

So when the liturgy prays that we might love God perfectly, it certainly means this much: that we will love as God loves. As one closing prayer puts it, "And now, Father, send us out to do the work you have given us to do." That work is nothing less than the work of creation, the creation of others in love.

To love God, of course, means more than doing what we've been called by him to do. It also means to enter into loving union with him. And since God is a Trinity-in-Love, it must mean that in some sense we become united with the Godhead, even mysteriously enter into the Three-in-One.

This sounds heretical until we remember how biblical the idea of union is. It is revealed by the little phrase "in Christ" or "in Jesus" (which appears over fifty times in Paul's writings), especially when it is used to describe our relationship to Christ. We hear language about being adopted *as sons and daughters* of the Father—little Christs. We read those passages about the Holy Spirit *dwelling* in us, as in Paul's monumental phrase: "Christ *in you,* the hope of glory." Peter gives us the most pregnant phrase, when he says that we become "partakers of the divine nature."

This is one thing that is happening when we participate in the liturgy, and especially when we partake of Christ's body and blood in the Eucharist. We are partaking of the divine nature.

The early church picked up this theme and summarized it simply: "God became man that we might become God." Granted, this is hyperbole, because we can't become divine in the sense that God is divine—the early church fathers knew that better than anyone. But they insisted on the dramatic language to drive home the mysterious and magnificent gospel that we can be united with the Trinity and the Trinity with us, that we can partake of the divine nature to such a degree that the original image and likeness of God in us shines forth in glory.

C.S. Lewis made the same point when he said, "It is a serious thing to live in a society of possible gods and goddesses, to remember that the dullest and most uninteresting person you talk to may one day be a creature which, if you saw it now, you would be strongly tempted to worship."

Our radical identification with God—God in us, we in God—our incorporation into the Godhead—this too is what it means to love God perfectly. And while the entire Christian life—prayer, study, service, spiritual disciplines, fellowship, and so forth—helps us live into our godliness, this calling is shaped mostly by the church's worship.

As one liturgical theologian put it, "The primary purpose of the Church's liturgical worship is not to express our feelings toward God, but to express and impress the Personality of Christ upon us." And therefore the personality of the Trinity upon us.

On *us*. Indeed, as individuals we are impressed upon. But through the liturgy, the Holy Spirit brings us not only into communion with Christ, but forms us into a body with others. "For this reason the Church is the great sacrament of divine communion," says the Catholic catechism, "which gathers God's scattered children together. Communion with the Holy Trinity and fraternal communion are inseparably the fruit of the Spirit in the liturgy."

To love God perfectly means this too—to enter into the communion of his people who together are shaped into Trinitarian life, where the centrifugal force of love accelerates until even more life and love fly off into being. We are loved and we love, and therefore we are.

CHAPTER 13

DRUNKEN SOBRIETY
How the Liturgy Helps us to Know God
with Imagination

THE LITURGY IS IMMEDIATELY ATTRACTIVE ON TWO
LEVELS.

It is attractive to the mind. There is a coherence, a logic, an order to the service that can engage us intellectually for a long time. This book has been an attempt to reveal some of the inner logic of the liturgy, to demonstrate that the riches found here are only the first inch of a thick vein that runs throughout the mountain of God.

The liturgy is also attractive to the heart. Who could not be moved by the mystical flickering of candles, the rich tapestry of color, the communal chanting of ancient prayers, and the participation in deeply symbolic acts?

But unless we're willing to enter into a knowledge that transcends mind and heart, we will soon find ourselves wandering from liturgy, and robbing ourselves of a profound knowledge of God. To be sure, this deeper knowledge can be enjoyed outside of liturgical worship, but in the liturgy we find poetry and theology and drama and mystery in a way that opens us up to transcendent knowledge in continually fresh ways.

The knowledge is not "knowledge" in the normal sense, for we tend to use that word to signal intellectual apprehension. Some people have called the type of knowledge the liturgy offers "imagination." Naturally, that word has its own weaknesses, because it signals that we're thinking of things that are not real, or not yet real. Liturgical imagination, though, means to apprehend that which is fully real but is incapable of being apprehended with the mind or heart alone.

C.S. Lewis spoke of imagination in this way when he wrote, "For me, reason is the natural organ of truth; but imagination is the organ of meaning." Commenting on this, Robert Houston Smith said:

> What he meant was that some aspects of reality cannot be conveyed except through imagination. Deeper realities transcend even the most abstract language, so that in the end, God cannot be comprehended by theological language alone. The imagination is one way to grasp higher levels of reality.

Some call this type of knowledge "spiritual intelligence," that is, a faculty that transcends and yet "unifies feeling and thought, body and soul, sensation and rationality. It is the kind of intelligence that sees the meaning in things." This type of knowledge Paul wants the Ephesians to have when he prays "that the God of our Lord Jesus Christ, the Father of glory, may give you a spirit of wisdom and of revelation in the knowledge of him."

It is also the knowledge that Paul points to when he writes in his first letter to Corinth:

> For who knows a person's thoughts except the spirit of that person, which is in him? So also no one comprehends the thoughts of God except the Spirit of God. Now we have received not the spirit of the world, but the Spirit

who is from God, that we might understand the things freely given us by God. (2:11–12)

Oxford scholar Stratford Caldecott aptly called it *sobria ebrietas* ("drunken" sobriety)—both "ecstatic, rapturous," and at the same time "measured, ordered, dignified. It is an encounter with the Other which takes the heart out of itself and places it in another center."

In other words, this is the "knowledge" the Bible usually talks about, deeply personal, so deep it is mysterious, so personal that it manifests love.

The phrase "drunken sobriety" gets right to the heart of why this type of knowledge is a stumbling block for us. "Drunken" suggests it is something out of our control. We are attracted to intellectual knowing precisely because we long to "master" a subject and get "control" of our material. To know God merely intellectually, though, is not so much to know God as to try to be God.

But it is also "sobriety," that is, something orderly and dignified. Though Paul could wax eloquent about our mystical relationship to Christ, and praise the use of the ecstatic gifts (like tongues), he nonetheless insisted that worship "be done decently and in order." Pure emotive worship does not lead to a genuine encounter with God any more than pure intellectual worship does.

Drunken sobriety combines the intellect and the heart, and yet transcends them, allowing us to enter into God's presence in a way that the mind and heart alone or together cannot. It is to love God with the soul's spiritual intelligence.

Soul intelligence is not easily developed. It requires years and years of practice, submitting oneself to spiritual disciplines and routines—the chief one being corporate worship. Liturgical worship, because it traffics in words and symbols and holy actions that not only point to God but manifest him, is an unparalleled gift to people who want to *know* God in the biblical sense, who want soul intelligence on top of the intelligence of mind and heart.

But years and years of practice requires perseverance. There will be long stretches when the liturgy feels like meaningless mumbo jumbo, when your entire being will call out for some fresh stimuli, when "the assurance of things hoped for, the conviction of things not seen" will abandon you.

I am not suggesting that there are no other salutary approaches to worship, that a healthy break in routine cannot be good for the soul. But for the liturgy to work it's "magic," for it to do its part in pulling out weeds of self-interest and nurturing the soul's intelligence, we must eschew impatience.

The cure for impatience is not patience, as much as we might think it is. Impatience, after all, is the original sin: W.H. Auden said, "Because of impatience we were driven out of Paradise, because of impatience we cannot return." As such, impatience cannot be cured by will power, by just trying to be patient. We are no longer capable, by our own powers, of anything but impatience.

Instead we need to return again to the fountain of faith, the Spirit; for patience, along with love, joy, and peace, is a fruit of the Spirit. In practical terms what this means is simple: when we enter into liturgical worship, we look to the Spirit, who has been sent by the Father to manifest his Son. We do not look for a particular religious experience. We do not look to be edified. We do not look to be instructed.

We look to God. We worship him, Father, Son, and Holy Spirit. We do this on weeks we feel the joy of the Lord. We do this on weeks we only feel despair. We do this on weeks we feel nothing. And if we do this for weeks and years, slowly we'll find that the soul is gaining its own sort of intelligence, that we're apprehending things the mind and heart cannot fathom, we're entering into the divine presence, and that divine presence is entering into us.

CHAPTER 14

WORDS OF LIVING W-A-T-E-R
The Liturgy as Poetic Reality that Transforms

O N A SPRING DAY IN 1887—"the most important day I can remember," she later said—a young girl just shy of seven years old learned the meaning of her first word: *water*.

After being struck with what was called at the time "brain fever" (probably scarlet fever) at the age of one and a half, Helen Keller was left deaf and blind. The world was mysterious, frustrating and maddening to her; she could make no sense of it. She quickly became a wild and unruly little girl, incapable of controlling her outbursts.

A twenty-year-old graduate of the Perkins School for the Blind, Anne Sullivan, was invited to the Keller home in Tuscumbia, Alabama, to become Helen's teacher. The family hoped Sullivan could somehow tame Helen.

Sullivan began by using hand language to spell words into Keller's hands. She started with d-o-l-l, hoping to connect the object with the letters. While Keller was bright and quickly learned how to spell a number of words, she didn't make the connection between the letters and the object. It was just mental gymnastics to her, until that spring day.

She and Sullivan had walked down a path to the wellhouse, where someone was drawing water. Sullivan placed a mug in Keller's hand and let the water fill and overflow. As the water gushed over the hand holding the mug, Sullivan spelled *water* in the other, first slowly, then rapidly.

Sullivan later recalled that Keller suddenly dropped the mug "and stood as one transfixed. A new light came to her face." Keller later described the moment by saying, "Suddenly I felt a misty consciousness as of something forgotten, a thrill of returning thought, and somehow the mystery of language was revealed to me."

It wasn't just the mystery of language, but the mystery of life that opened to her: "I knew then that 'w-a-t-e-r' meant the wonderful cool something that was flowing over my hand," she wrote. "That living word awakened my soul, gave it light, hope, joy, set it free!"

When our soul first awakens, it is words that awaken it, giving us light, hope and joy—from the first words of our parents, to the revelatory words of Scripture, to all words between, like the words we find in the liturgy. As the Gospel writer John said, "In the beginning was the Word." This is a statement not only about the eternity of the Son, but also the existential reality of our lives.

In a media age, words come at us from all directions, like arrows from a thousand bows. Most of these arrows are marketing words, advertising words, words designed to manipulate us, to sell us something.

In a political context, words often become a way not to reveal but to hide the truth. As George Orwell put it in his famous 1946 essay, "Politics of the English Language":

> In our time, political speech and writing are largely the defense of the indefensible. Things like the continuance of British rule in India, the Russian purges and deportations, the dropping of the atom bombs on Japan, can indeed

be defended, but only by arguments which are too brutal for most people to face, and which do not square with the professed aims of the political parties. Thus political language has to consist largely of euphemism, question-begging and sheer cloudy vagueness.

Change the examples in the middle of that paragraph, and the sense rings true today.

For these reasons, among others, we distrust words, especially words that have been fashioned and shaped for the occasion by Madison or Pennsylvania Avenue.

So it's not surprising that many are put off by the words of the liturgy. Surely, if we're trying to worship sincerely, praise a God who loves us as a father loves his children, we want to use language that is "authentic." What child uses formal speech to communicate with their "daddy"? We want nothing to do with pretension, stuffiness, and any rhetoric that prevents us from being real.

In our desire to be real, we start thinking that authenticity is another word for spontaneity, as if everything we say at the spur of the moment is more true, more sincere than words we craft carefully. For many, the Freudian slip is considered more authentic than the measured reply.

Indeed, sometimes what we blurt out thoughtlessly is actually what we mean and feel. But more often than not, what we blurt out is ill-considered and something we either need to qualify or apologize for.

The liturgy's answer to crafted language that deceives or manipulates is not to abandon crafted language but to shape it so that it reveals reality. The most carefully crafted language in our culture tends to be poetry. And poetry at its finest moments subverts our best attempts at hiding from reality. "Poetry may make us from time to time a little more aware of the deeper, unnamed feelings which form the substratum of our being, to which we rarely penetrate," said T.S. Eliot, "for our lives are mostly a constant evasion of ourselves."

The poetry of liturgy has just this power. The liturgy contains words that have been shaped and crafted over the centuries. It is formal speech. It is public poetry. As such it reaches into us to reveal not only the unnamed reality of our lives but the God who created us. "In worship the voice of the Church calls up thoughts and feelings often far beyond us," wrote one liturgical theologian, "yet to which something in us faintly but firmly responds."

The liturgy can call up those thoughts and feelings "far beyond us" because it traffics in biblical language. "For the word of God is living and active, sharper than any two-edged sword, piercing to the division of soul and of spirit, of joints and of marrow, and discerning the thoughts and intentions of the heart." But even when the words of the liturgy are not literally biblical, the words, like all truthful words, work on us over time, like a steady, unrelenting stream slowly reshapes the banks of a river. The words do something to us even when we're not paying attention.

About a year ago, I began using the Trisagion Prayers of the Orthodox tradition to begin my day. As I've noted, the liturgy of public worship takes the same overall shape in a variety of traditions. Within those traditions we find unique contributions to the larger library of liturgical prayer, and I like to raid those various traditions from time to time. They are not universal in the same way the public, Sunday liturgy is; these unique liturgical traditions may not be found in other liturgical communions. But they are universal in that they work on us in the same way that the common traditions do—calling us into the community of the Trinity and the Church, transforming us into Christlikeness. Furthermore, I like to remember that whenever I personally pray from any liturgical tradition, I am nonetheless praying with members of that tradition, those present and those who have gone before me.

The Trisagion is one of the unique contributions of the Orthodox tradition. I began using it because it exalts the majesty of God in a way that seems fitting—"Holy God, Holy Mighty, Holy Immortal, have mercy on us" being one phrase from these prayers. So, updating some of the language to modern English, I began praying:

> O heavenly King, O Comforter, the Spirit of truth; you are in all places and fill all things; Treasury of good things and Giver of life: Come and dwell in us and cleanse us from every stain, and save our souls, O gracious Lord.

And,

> All-holy Trinity, have mercy on us. Lord, cleanse us from our sins. Master, pardon our iniquities. Holy God, visit and heal our infirmities for your Name's sake.

I shouldn't have been surprised—though I was—that repeatedly praying "cleanse us from every stain," and "cleanse us from our sins," and "visit and heal our infirmities" would after a few months pull up from my subconscious not only various and sundry sins I had not been aware of, or unaware of for some time, but also a deeper recognition of the depth of my sinfulness. I employed the prayers to ground myself ever more profoundly in the majesty of God, but the penitential aspect of the prayers worked on me without my conscious effort.

I have also made regular use of the service called Morning Prayer in the Book of Common Prayer, especially the General Thanksgiving:

> Almighty God, Father of all mercies,
> we your unworthy servants give you humble thanks
> for all your goodness and loving-kindness
> to us and to all whom you have made.
> We bless you for our creation, preservation,
> and all the blessings of this life;
> but above all for your immeasurable love
> in the redemption of the world by our Lord Jesus Christ;
> for the means of grace, and for the hope of glory.
> And, we pray, give us such an awareness of your mercies,
> that with truly thankful hearts we may show forth your
>   praise,
> not only with our lips, but in our lives,
> by giving up our selves to your service,
> and by walking before you
> in holiness and righteousness all our days;

through Jesus Christ our Lord,
to whom, with you and the Holy Spirit,
be honor and glory throughout all ages. Amen.

This is a striking bit of prayer poetry. The cadence of the lines pulls one along, as if drawn by the Holy Spirit into a broader river of new life. The words condense the magnificent sweep of salvation history, and put an exclamation point ("your immeasurable love") on the coming of Christ. It sets the life of holiness in the context of thanksgiving and service. This liturgical prayer says everything that needs to be said, and shapes me in a way that I believe God is calling me to be shaped—to walk in holiness and righteousness all my days.

"We human beings are, as the late Abraham Heschel insisted, the cantors of the universe," writes Richard John Neuhaus. "And language is our instrument. Language is not to be seen in a purely instrumental way, however. Language is to be celebrated. And the better it is celebrated, not so oddly, the more effective an instrument it will be for the praise of God and the edification of his people."

Indeed, the finely tuned language of liturgy has an edifying end, but the point of liturgical poetry is not merely pragmatic. Language that is beautiful may be useful and truthful, but the beauty is "useless" in some respects, and harkens to something beyond what it *does* for us. As we prepare for a dinner guest, we set a beautiful table and decorate it with flowers. It is not something that is practical or necessary. But we do it nonetheless out of love.

The words of the liturgy, of course, are more than a beautiful tablecloth and flowers. They constitute even the meal itself. This is the feast to which we are invited in the Gathering, at which the host speaks to us in his Word, during which we are sustained by the Eucharist, from which we are sent forth in the Dismissal to gather others into the community of the Trinity and the Church, who now together anticipate the great forever feast in the kingdom that comes.

ACKNOWLEDGMENTS

F RIENDS who critiqued chapters include Matt Pechanio, Stephen Gauthier, and Erik Olsen. Their comments have proved invaluable.

Parts of some chapters have appeared in a bi-weekly column "SoulWork" that appears on *Christianity Today Online.* Comments about those columns, especially those expressed on my blog—www.markgalli.com/galliblog—have also shaped the final product.

The liturgical life of St. Mark's Episcopal Church, Glen Ellyn, Illinois, and Church of the Resurrection, Wheaton, Illinois, have not only shaped this book but my life in ways I can hardly begin to recount. I remain deeply grateful for the pastoral and liturgical leadership of the reverends Ray Cole, Chip Edgar, and Stewart Ruch.

Lil Copan, my editor at Paraclete, has done just what I had hoped—affirmed my writing when it has gone well, and firmly put me on a course correction when it hasn't. Sr. Mercy and Ron Minor, other editors at Paraclete, have fine-tuned the final product so that it is an even smoother read.

Finally, my wife, Barbara, has once again remained an understanding spouse throughout the writing of another book. Without her emotional and intellectual support, I could not pursue this avocation.

A LITURGY PRIMER

A s NOTED IN CHAPTER 1, *liturgy* comes from a Greek word meaning "a public service." When I refer to "the liturgy" in this book, I mostly mean the public Sunday service performed by liturgical and mainline churches. I refer to it in the singular because the shape of the service is remarkably similar in all these traditions.

Liturgical theologian Frank Senn wrote, "It has been said that if the covers were removed from the major worship books of the late twentieth century, it would be difficult to tell which book belongs to which church body." This is an exaggeration, as Senn notes, but it is nonetheless surprising how common is the shape of the liturgy in the major traditions of the West. See Appendix B to note how all five—Roman Catholic, Lutheran, Anglican, Methodist, and Presbyterian—follow the four-act structure of Gathering, Word, Sacrament, and Dismissal. Some simplify the service by formally dividing it into just two acts (Word and Sacrament), but Gathering and Dismissal are very much a part of each service.

If you are reading this book, you are most likely already attending a liturgical church, and thus have access to its liturgical books, certainly its service for Sunday morning. Pastors and priests in that tradition are the experts in that tradition and can point you to the various and sundry liturgical books that might be helpful.

If you are not already worshiping in a liturgical church, the best place to begin an experiment in liturgical spirituality is to attend such a church. You can indeed buy a Lutheran or Roman Catholic or Anglican prayer book and pray by yourself, but the private praying of liturgy is but a supplement to the corporate liturgy. The public worship of God with others is the place to begin if you are going to grasp and be shaped by the liturgy.

Let me take the order of the tradition I'm most familiar with (an Anglican order used in my parish) and note quickly the meaning and place of each part of a typical service. Naturally, depending on the day of the church year, there will be variations. Note also how even this outline is slightly different than the one suggested in the graph in Appendix B, but also how it nonetheless accords to the larger shape of modern liturgy.

Gathering

Opening Hymn, Psalm, Anthem: As noted, unified voices of the congregation (or that of the choir on behalf of the congregation) gather us into a body as we praise God for, among other things, his gathering us to himself.

Acclamation: We proclaim in whose name we have come (Father, Son, and Holy Spirit), and the scope of his mercies (extending to the kingdom).

Collect for Purity: This prayer "collects" into itself the prayers of the church as it gathers for worship—that we may "worthily magnify your Holy Name."

Gloria: A traditional hymn of praise.

Word

Collect of the Day: This prayer "collects," or summarizes, the theme of the Scripture readings for the day, and thus acts as a transition from Gathering to Word.

The Lessons: Readings from the Old Testament and the New Testament epistles, with a reading of a psalm between. Though the psalm is Scripture, its use in the liturgy tends to be more like that of a hymn or prayer.

The Gospel is usually the last reading, with the congregation standing to hear it. It is often framed by the singing of an Alleluia, and sometimes incense and a procession to the midst of the congregation. Such is the reverence we have for the very words and/or acts of Jesus, the Incarnate Word.

The Sermon: Traditionally an exposition of one of the readings, usually the Gospel. But it can be based on another Scripture passage altogether.

The Nicene Creed: A summary of the entire faith, a faith that the lessons and the sermon have just delved into.

Prayers of the People: In response to the Word, we offer our petitions to God for the church, the nation, the world, the local community, the suffering, and the departed.

Confession of Sin: Also in response to the Word, we confess those areas of our lives that fall short of God's Word to us.

The Peace: This is a transition to the Eucharist. We are commanded by our Lord (Matthew 5:23–24) to be at peace with our brothers and sisters before we offer our gift in worship. The offering of this peace is not merely a way to greet others in worship but is an enacted symbol of our need to be reconciled with one another in Christ.

Eucharist

The Offertory: In anticipation of the Eucharist, we offer our gifts to God, including the bread and wine that will be consecrated.

The Great Prayer of Thanksgiving: It includes a greeting in the name of the Lord, another collect that sums up the day's theme, a hymn of praise called the *Sanctus*, and a rehearsal of the great acts of God in history.

The Lord's Prayer: The early church identified the phrase "our daily bread" as a reference to the bread of Communion, thus since the fifth century, this prayer has been seen as preparation to receive the Sacrament.

The Breaking of Bread and Communion: We partake of the body and blood of Christ, sometimes accompanied by another prayer of preparation (called the Prayer of Humble Access) and/or an anthem of the same purpose.

Dismissal

Postcommunion Prayer: This prayer thanks God for the gift of himself in the Eucharist, and asks for the ability to love and serve God in the world.

The Blessing: A final call to go out in the name of Christ, with an acclamation of thanksgiving.

I have noted only the more prominent movements in the liturgy, but there are movements within movements. For instance, the Great Prayer of Thanksgiving can be divided into the opening dialogue, the praise and thanksgiving, the *Sanctus*, the *Benedictus qui venit,* the institution narrative, the memorial acclamation, and others. It is all very interesting to liturgical theologians, and it is very possible to miss the liturgical forest for the trees and branches of the service.

We are wiser, at the beginning, to not worry about what each and every part means—its history and theology and exact place in the service. As one priest instructed me, when the service becomes too confusing, just put down the prayer book and let the church around you pray for you. And simply listen. The liturgy is a grand story with too many details to master in short order. Better to let the larger drama sweep over you and let the details come as they will.

LITURGY COMPARED ACROSS TRADITIONS

ROMAN MISSAL 1969	LUTHERAN BOOK OF WORSHIP 1978	BOOK OF COMMON PRAYER 1979 (ANGLICAN)
The Order of Mass	*The Holy Communion*	*The Holy Eucharist*
Entrance Psalm	(Brief Order for Confession)	(Hymn, Psalm, or Anthem)
Invocation and Greeting		(Penitential Rite)
	Entrance Hymn	(Hymn, Psalm, or Anthem)
Penitential Rite	Apostolic Greeting	
(Kyrie)	(Kyrie)	Greeting and Collect
(Gloria)	(Gloria or Worthy is Christ, or Hymn)	(Gloria or Kyrie or Trisagion)
Salutation and Collect for the Day	Salutation and Prayer for the Day	Salutation and Collect for the Day
First Lesson	First Lesson	First Lesson
Psalmody	Psalmody	(Hymn, Psalm, or Anthem)
Second Lesson	Second Lesson	Second Lesson
Alleluia Verse	Alleluia Verse	(Hymn, Psalm, or Anthem)
Gospel	Gospel	Gospel
Homily	Sermon	Sermon
Nicene Creed	Nicene or Apostle's Creed	Nicene Creed
Intercessions	Prayers of the Church	Prayers of the People
Offering	(Confession of Sin)	(Confession of Sin)
Offertory Song	Greeting of Peace	The Peace
Offertory Prayers	Offering	Offertory Sentence
Preface and Sanctus	Offertory Verse	Offertory Procession
Canon (9 options)	Offertory Prayer	
	Preface and Sanctus	Preface and Sanctus
Lord's Prayer	Great Thanksgiving (5 options)	Great Thanksgiving (4 options)
Peace of the Lord	or Words of Institution	
Lamb of God	Lord's Prayer	
Communion		Lord's Prayer
(Communion songs)	Communion	Breaking of the Bread
Silent Reflection	Lamb of God or other hymns	Communion
Post-Communion Prayer	Post-Communion song	(Hymn, Psalm, or Anthem)
	Post-Communion Prayer	
Benediction and Dismissal	Silent Reflection	Post-Communion Prayer
	Benediction and Dismissal	Benediction and Dismissal

THE METHODIST HYMNAL 1989	BOOK OF COMMON WORSHIP 1993 (PRESBYTERIAN)
Service of Word and Table	*Service for the Lord's Day*
Gathering	Call to Worship
Greeting	Prayer of the Day
Hymn of Praise	Hymn of Praise
Opening Prayer	Confession and Pardon
	(The Peace)
(Act of Praise)	Canticle: Psalm, Hymn, or Spiritual
Prayer for Illumination	Prayer for Illumination
Scripture Lesson	First Reading
(Psalm)	Psalm
(Scripture Lesson)	Second Reading
Hymn or Song	(Anthem, Hymn, Psalm, Canticle,
	or Spiritual)
Gospel Lesson	Gospel Reading
Sermon	Sermon
(Occasional Service)	
The Apostle's Creed	Affirmation of Faith
Concerns and Prayers	(Pastoral Rite of the Church)
Invitation to the Table	Prayers of the People
Confession and Pardon	
The Peace	(The Peace)
Offering	Offering
(Hymn, Psalm, or Anthem)	
	Invitation to the Table
Great Thanksgiving	Great Thanksgiving
The Lord's Prayer	Lord's Prayer
Breaking of Bread	Breaking of Bread
Giving the Bread and Cup	Communion of the People
Post-Communion Prayer	Hymn, Spiritual, Canticle, or Psalm
Hymn or Song	
	Charge and Blessing
Dismissal with Blessing	
Going Forth	

THE CHRISTIAN YEAR

THE CHRISTIAN YEAR consists of the cycle of liturgical seasons that determine when festival days (also called feasts, memorials, commemorations, or solemnities, depending on the tradition) are observed, which portions of Scripture are read, and which prayers are prayed.

For example, during Advent, when the first and second coming of Christ is the focus, the Scripture readings will highlight his birth and his second coming. During Lent, the penitential season that prepares us for Easter and resurrection, the readings and prayers will accent the themes of repentance.

In addition, distinct liturgical colors (displayed in the priest or minister's dress, in cloth hangings around the altar or pulpit, and so forth) may appear in connection with different seasons of the liturgical year. For example, purple is the color for Advent and Lent, white for Christmas and Easter, and red for the day of Pentecost. The dates of the festivals vary somewhat between the Western (Roman Catholic, Anglican, Lutheran, and Protestant) Churches and the Eastern Orthodox Churches, though the sequence and logic is the same.

The Christian calendar has its roots in the Jewish calendar, whose rhythm is grounded both weekly ("Remember the Sabbath day, to keep it holy. Six days you shall labor, and do all your work, but the seventh day is a Sabbath to the LORD your God") and annually ("Three times in the year you shall keep a feast to me") Jesus himself celebrated both this weekly (he attended Sabbath worship "as was his habit") and annual calendar (in John's Gospel, Jesus attended Passover three times). The early disciples did not change this pattern, and we find them gathering for prayer during the Jewish Day of Pentecost, when the Holy Spirit descended on them with power.

It was only natural that, in light of the new creation in Christ, Christians would begin to rethink their sense of time. Since Sunday was the day of Christ's resurrection, which inaugurates the new era, Sunday worship became the hinge of the weekly calendar. It spoke both to the past and to the future kingdom. Sunday was considered the first day of the week, and the eighth day—the beginning and culmination of history.

Early Christians also began to rethink the year. One of the earliest and most intense controversies of the church was over setting the annual date of Easter. Should it be celebrated on the same *date* each year, no matter on what day of the week it falls? Or should it always be celebrated on a Sunday? And if the latter, which Sunday?

This may seem silly to us, because we tend to think of the annual calendar as merely a way to mark the passing of time based on the earth's annual revolution around the sun. The early Christians knew that a calendar not only marks time but does something to us, so getting it right was no small matter. They worked hard to settle the matter.

As the centuries unfolded, it became clear that other events crucial to the new creation should be celebrated annually, and eventually the full "church year" came into being.

The church year begins not on January 1 but with the season of Advent, from the Latin *adventus*, "arrival" or "coming." The season begins four Sundays before Christmas and concludes on Christmas Eve. Historically observed as a penitential season (a "fast"), the prayers and readings prepare us for the coming Christ. Although often conceived as awaiting the Christ-child of Christmas, the modern lectionary points us toward eschatological themes—awaiting the final coming of Christ, when "the wolf shall dwell with the lamb" (Isaiah 11:6a) and when God will have "brought down the mighty from their thrones and exalted those of humble estate" (the Magnificat, Luke 1:52)—particularly in the earlier half of the season.

Christmastide begins the evening of Christmas Eve (December 24) and concludes on the Feast of the Epiphany (January 6). Christmas Day is December 25. "The Twelve Days of Christmas" begin on Christmas Day.

Epiphany (from the Greek word for "appearance" or "manifestation") celebrates the revelation of God in human form, in the person of Jesus. The season of Epiphany lasts until Ash Wednesday, when the season of Lent begins.

Lent is a major season for fasting, during which the prayers and readings prepare us for Easter. It begins on Ash Wednesday and ends on Palm Sunday, the beginning of Holy Week. There are forty days of Lent, counting from Ash Wednesday through Palm Sunday, excluding Sundays.

Holy Week includes Maundy Thursday, Good Friday, Holy Saturday (days to remember the suffering and death of Christ), and culminates with the Easter Vigil, which celebrates Christ's resurrection.

The season of Easter begins on the Sunday of the Resurrection, Pascha, or Resurrection Day, the most important religious feast of the Christian liturgical year. It is observed at some point between late March and late April each year (early April to early May in Eastern Christianity) and extends to Pentecost.

Pentecost is celebrated the fiftieth day after Easter Sunday. It is related to the Jewish harvest festival of Shavuot, but for Christians it commemorates the descent of the Holy Spirit upon the Apostles and other followers of Jesus. Pentecost is also called Whitsun, Whitsunday, or Whit Sunday in the United Kingdom and other English-speaking areas. It lasts until a new church year begins with another Advent (this period is also called Ordinary Time in some traditions).

Since the date of Christmas is fixed on December 25, the four weeks of Advent are fixed. All the other seasons orbit around Easter, and thus are in part or in whole "movable." Holy Week is the week before Easter. Lent is begins forty days before Holy Week. Epiphany, while beginning after the twelve days of Christmas, ends whenever Lent begins. Pentecost begins fifty days after Easter. So depending on when Easter begins, these other seasons will have different starting and/or ending dates.

All that being said, it is not important to know exactly when these seasons begin and end, or what exctly to pray and read during each season. That is why we have the body of Christ and liturgical tradition. We just step into the season that the church is celebrating, and let the church guide our hearts and minds as we worship.

NOTES

INTRODUCTION

9   *And we all, with unveiled face* 2 Corinthians 3:18.

For the Life of the World: Sacraments and Orthodoxy (Crestwood, NY: St. Vladimir's Press, 2002).

1,000 to 2,000 new religious movements were formed in the United States James Herrick, *The Making of the New Spirituality: The Eclipse of Western Religious Tradition* (Downers Grove, IL: InterVarsity Press, 2003), 17.

10   *an eclectic mix of religious and spiritual ideas and practices.* From *Spiritual Marketplace: Baby Boomers and the Remaking of American Religion* (Princeton, NJ: Princeton University Press, 2001), as quoted in James Herrick, *The Making of the New Spirituality,* 18.

various forms of psychotherapy Leigh Schmidt, *Restless Souls: The Making of American Spirituality* (San Franciscio: HarperSanFrancisco, 2005).

The benefits far surpass those of psychotherapy Colleen Carroll Campbell, *The New Faithful: Why Young Adults Are Embracing Christian Orthodoxy* (Chicago: Loyola Press, 2002), 3.

CHAPTER 1

15   *Let the redeemed of the LORD say so* Psalm 107:2–3.

On this mountain the LORD of hosts Isaiah 25:6.

Blessed be God, Father, Son, and Holy Spirit Book of Common Prayer [BCP] (New York: Church Hymnal Corporation, 1979), 355.

17   *And now the Lord says* Isaiah 49:5.

18   *We are the people sent forth*   This enables us to see how the liturgy helps transform one of our natural instincts. How often, in frustration with the church, I have thought, *I just want to go off and worship by myself, out in a garden or some scenic spot.* But *worship,* it turns out, is primarily about the *gathering* of a people to feast *together* in the presence of a *communal,* Trinitarian God. While private prayer is an essential part of the spiritual journey, *worship* is something different, something grand and large and inclusive. More of these themes later in the book.

    The Eucharist is celebrated in thanksgiving   Jeremy Driscoll, *What Happens at Mass* (Chicago: Liturgy Training Publications, 2005), 10.

CHAPTER 2

23   *April is the cruelest month*   T.S. Eliot, *The Waste Land*, Norton Critical Edition (New York: W.W. Norton and Company, 2000). Poem originally published in 1922.

    And God said, "Let there be lights"   Genesis 1:14.

24   *The date of Easter*   This was a political compromise reached at the Council of Nicea in 325 between lunar and solar calendar advocates (the details of which are too complex to go into here). For a succinct and engaging explanation, see the article, "Why Does the Date of Easter Wander?" by Farrell Brown, on the *Christian History & Biography* Web site: www.christianitytoday. com/history/newsletter/2004/apr9a.html.

25   *In the Son, time co-exists*   Joseph Cardinal Ratzinger *The Spirit of the Liturgy,* translated by John Saward (San Francisco: Ignatius Press, 2000), 94 and 92, respectively.

    I do not ask that you take them   John 17:15–18.

26   *We are heirs of your eternal kingdom*   BCP, 366. Emphasis added.

    So teach us to number our days   Psalm 90:12.

CHAPTER 3

29   *For you alone are the Holy One*   BCP, 356.

30   *Sheila Larson is a young nurse*   From a lecture by Robert Bellah, "Habits of the Heart: Implications for Religion." From the Robert N. Bellah Web site, copyright by the Hartford Institute for Religious Research: http://www.robertbellah.com/lectures_5.htm.

33   *Heavenly Father, in you we live*   BCP, 100.
     Most merciful God BCP, 79.

35   *the goal, the end of all our desires and interests*   Alexander Schmemann, *For the Life of the World* (Crestwood NY, St. Vladimir's Press, 2002), 29.

36   *I confess to almighty God*   From the Roman Missal (1970), in the section "Liturgy of the Word," "Penitential Rite." From Catholic Liturgy Library Web site, http://www.catholicliturgy.com/index.cfm/FuseAction/Text/Index/4/SubIndex/67/ContentIndex/10/Start/9.
     Sanctify us also that we may faithfully   BCP, 363, emphasis added.
     They have been individuals   For the Life of the World, 27.

37   *So then you are no longer strangers and aliens*   Ephesians 2:19.

CHAPTER 4

39   *One day I stared at her across the kitchen table*   Adapted from an article I originally wrote for *Marriage Partnership* (Winter 2004), "Irreconcilable Differences—So?" that can now be found at http://www.christianitytoday.com/mp/2004/004/1.36.html.

40   *Heaven is part of the created world*   Karl Barth, *Prayer and Preaching* (London: SCM Press, 1964), 27.

41   *the Lord sitting upon a throne*   Isaiah 6:1–3.
     over their heads there was the likeness of a throne   Ezekiel 1:26–29.

43   *And the Word became flesh*   John 1:14.

44   *I have been crucified with Christ,*   Galatians 2:20.
     Christ in you,   Colossians 1:27.

45   *Hear us, O merciful Father*   *The United Methodist Book of Worship*
     (Nashville, TN: The United Methodist Publishing House,
     1992), "Service of Word and Table IV," page 48.

CHAPTER 5

47   *We value God-honoring, understandable worship*   North
     Valley Baptist Church, Mayfield, Pennsylvania: http://www.
     northvalleych.com/About%20Us%20Menu.htm.

     For one who speaks in a tongue   1 Corinthians 14:2.

48   *Remembering, therefore, his salutary command*   *Evangelical Lutheran
     Worship* (Minneapolis: Augsburg Fortress, 2006) page 5.

49   *To know him really is to know him as unknowable*   Meister
     Eckhart, C. de B. Evans, vol. 1, sermon on "The Divine Being"
     (London: John M. Watkins, 1956), 53–55.

     Left to ourselves we tend immediately   A.W. Tozer, *Knowledge of
     the Holy: The Attributes of God: Their Meaning in the Christian
     Life* (New York: Harper & Brothers, 1961), 16.

51   *The word mystery preserves the tension*   Driscoll, *What happens
     at Mass*, 4.

53   *People just coming to the church*   Ibid., 8.
     The heavens declare the glory of God   Psalm 19:1.
     For his invisible attributes   Romans 1:20.

CHAPTER 6

55   *A recent book on "the missional church"*   Michael Frost and Alan
     Hirsch, *The Shaping of Things to Come* (Grand Rapids, MI:
     Hendrickson, 2003), xi.

56   *Relevant is a casual*   See http://www.relevantchurch.com.

    make Christianity understandable *For the Life of the World: Sacraments and Orthodoxy* (Crestwood, NY: St. Vladimir Press, 2002) p.27.

58   *I don't think people care a whole lot* Eugene Peterson "Spirituality for All the Wrong Reasons," interview by Mark Galli, *Christianity Today* 49, no. 3 (March 2005), 47.

59   *Celebrant: Blessed be God* BCP, 355, 366.

61   *The grandeur of the liturgy* "Remarks to the Bishops of Chile Regarding the Lefebvre Schism, July 13, 1988." From the Una Voce America Web site: http://www.unavoce.org

    When he was at table with them Luke 24:30–31.

    The one who hears you hears me Luke 10:16a.

62   *very meet, right, and our bounden duty* BCP, Holy Eucharist 1, 333.

    And on the day called Sunday   Justin Martyr, *The First Apology,* From *St. Justin Martyr: The First and Second Apologies,* translated by Leslie William Barnard (New York: Paulist Press, 1997), 71. An online version can be found at http://www.ccel.org/ccel/schaff/anf01.viii.ii.lxvii.html.

63   *All liturgical acts* F.H. Brabant, "Worship in General," in *Liturgy and Worship: A Companion to the Prayer Books of the Anglican Communion,* edited by W.K. Lowther Clark, with the assistance of Charles Harris (London: SPCK, 1954), 12.

CHAPTER 7

65   *Holy, holy, holy is the Lord of hosts* Isaiah 6:3.

66   *Holy, holy, holy* Revelation 4:8b.

67   *Then the angel showed me*   Revelation 22:1–2a.

68   *slavery nurtures in you the shoots* Aleksandr I. Solzhenitsyn, *The Gulag Archipelago 1918–1956: An Experiment in Literary*

Investigation III and IV (New York: Harper & Row, 1973), 610–11.
Bless you, Prison! Ibid., 617.

CHAPTER 8

71   *And Jacob set up a pillar*   Genesis 35:14–15.

73   *For in the Eucharist*   Driscoll, *What Happens at Mass*, 9.

With the whole people   *Lutheran Book of Worship* (Minneapolis: Augsburg Fortress Publishers, 1978), the beginning of prayer of intercession, in the section called Service of the Word, 7.

74   *great cloud of witnesses*   Hebrews 12:1.

And therefore we praise you   BCP, Eucharistic Prayer C, 370.

75   *A worshiper at the Brotherhood of St. George.*   Amy Johnson Frykholm, "Smells and Bells: Turning to Orthodoxy," 1st line of story from *Christian Century,* December 28, 2004, 18.

CHAPTER 9

77   *I've played because*   Melissa King, *She's Got Next: A Story of Getting In, Staying Open, and Taking a Shot* (New York: Houghton Mifflin, 2005), iii.

time seems to slow way down   As quoted in Michael Murphy, *The Psychic Side of Sports* (Reading, MA: Addison-Wesley Publishing Company, 1979), 46.

79   *Nothing can stop the man*   See http://thinkexist.com/quotes and www.brainyquote.com/quotes/ among many other quote sites.

81   *It is an Emmaus-like experience*   Richard John Neuhaus, *Freedom for Ministry: A Critical Affirmation of the Church and Its Mission* (New York: Harper & Row, 1979), 143.

82   *Whoever feeds on my flesh*   John 6:56.

Where two or three are gathered Matthew 18:20.

The Church is Christ Quoted in Simon Chan, *Liturgical Theology: The Church as Worshiping Community* (Downers Grove, IL: InterVarsity Press, 2006), 27.

CHAPTER 10

83 *Who will deliver me* Romans 7:24.

86 *the water of Baptism* BCP, 306.

The Body of Christ BCP, 365.

87 *Bring no more vain offerings* Isaiah 1:13–14.

88 *This is why the [L]iturgy* Brabant, "Worship in General," 13.

Being unwilling to bend Bishop Thomas Olmsted, "Knees to Love Christ," *Adoremus Bulletin,* online ed., II, no. 3, May 2005, http://www.adoremus.org/0505Olmsted_Kneeling.html. Originally published *The Catholic Sun,* February 17 and March 3, 2005.

CHAPTER 11

91 *To understand how* The following discussion of epistemology is indebted to a *Theology Today* (October 2001) essay, "Worship as Catechesis: Knowledge, Desire, and Christian Formation," by Debra Dean Murphy, which can be found at http://www.findarticles.com/p/articles/mi_qa3664/is_200110/ai_n8958098.

92 *that the God of our Lord Jesus Christ* Ephesians 1:17–19.

95 *Worship is first and finally* Robert Webber and Rodney Clapp, *People of the Truth* (San Francisco: Harper & Row, 1988), 69.

96 *The liturgy, like the feast* Aidan Kavanaugh, *Elements of Rite: A Handbook of Liturgical Style* (New York: Pueblo Publishing Company, 1982), 28.

CHAPTER 12

99 *The glory that you have given me*   John 17:22–23, 26.

100 *If you had known me*   John 14:7, 9, 11;16:13–14.

103 *And now Father*   BCP, 366.

104 *Christ in you,* Colossians 1:27b.

partakers of the divine nature   2 Peter 1:4.

It is a serious thing   C.S. Lewis, *The Weight of Glory* (San Francisco: HarperOne, 2001), 45. The sermon "The Weight of Glory" was originally preached in the Church of St. Mary the Virgin, Oxford, on June 8, 1942, and published in *Theology,* November, 1941, and by SPCK in 1942. See http://www. doxaweb.com/assets/doxa.pdf.

105 *The primary purpose*   Father Christopher Maxwell-Stewart "Liturgy: What Does It Mean?" on the EWTN Web site: http:// www.ewtn.com/library/liturgy/whatmean.txt

The article was originally published in the July 1996 issue of *Faith Magazine* (The Faith-Keyway Trust).

For this reason the Church   *Catechism of the Catholic Church* (Ligouri, MO: Ligouri Publications, 1994), paragraph 1108.

CHAPTER 13

107 *For me, reason is the natural organ*   Robert Houston Smith, *Patches of Godlight: The Pattern of Thought of C.S. Lewis* (Athens: University of Georgia Press, 1981), 136. Originally from the Lewis essay "Bluspels and Flalansferes," in C.S. Lewis, *Selected Literary Essays,* edited by Walter Hooper (Cambridge, England: Cambridge University Press, 1969) 265.

Some call this type of knowledge   Stratford Caldecott, "Liturgy and Trinity: Toward an Anthropology of the Liturgy," *Oriens,* 8, no. 1 (Winter 2002). Online at http://www.oriensjournal. com/12library.html.

that the God of our Lord Jesus Christ Ephesians 1:17.

108 *be done decently* 1 Corinthians 14:40.

109 *the assurance of things hoped for* Hebrews 11:1.

CHAPTER 14

112 *That living word awakened my soul* Helen Keller, *The Story of My Life,* Part 1, chapter 4, and Part III, "A Supplementary Account of Helen Keller's Life and Education, Including Passages from the Reports and Letters of Her Teacher, Anne Mansfield Sullivan," by John Albert Macy. Online at http://www.afb.org/mylife/book.asp?cg=P1Ch4 and http://www.afb.org/mylife/book.asp?ch=P3Ch3#7 respectively. Copyright 2003, The American Federation for the Blind.

In our time, political speech Online at http://www.orwell.ru/library/essays/politics/english/e_polit. This essay can be found in many places on the web. This quote is from Dag's Orwell Project, a site featuring a large selection of essays and texts of his novels in English and Russian: http://www.orwell.ru/home.html.

114 *Poetry may make us* T.S. Eliot, as quoted by Anders Österling in his 1948 Noble Prize in Literature Presenation Speech, Permanent Secretary of the Swedish Academy: http://nobelprize.org/nobel_prizes/literature/laureates/1948/press.html.

In worship the voice of the Church Brabant, "Worship in General," 15.

For the word of God Hebrews 4:12.

116 *Almighty God, Father of all mercies* BCP, 101.

117 *We human beings are* Richard John Neuhaus, *Freedom for Ministry: A Critical Affirmation of the Church and Its Mission* (New York: Harper & Row, 1979), 157.

APPENDIX A

121 *It has been said* Frank Senn, *Christian Liturgy: Catholic and Evangelical* (Minneapolis: Fortress Press, 1997), 645.

122 *or that of the choir* Whenever the choir sings, it does so *on behalf of the congregation.* It is not a performance *for* the congregation but represents the entire congregation, giving God praise that requires extra preparation and/or expertise.

APPENDIX B

126 *Liturgy Compared Across Traditions* This chart is taken from Senn, *Christian Liturgy*, 646–47.

APPENDIX C

129 *Six days you shall labor* Exodus 20:8–10.

   Three times in the year Exodus 23:14.

130 *Sunday was considered* Ratzinger, *The Spirit of the Liturgy,* 96.

   They worked hard Early Christians eventually settled on this seemingly strange formula: the first Sunday after the first full moon on or after the vernal equinox. This doesn't mean that today all Christians celebrate Easter on the same day. Western Christians and Eastern Orthodox Christians still find themselves celebrating Easter on different days because the Eastern Church—for historical and missional reasons—still uses the Gregorian Calendar, while the West follows the Julian Calendar.

ABOUT PARACLETE PRESS

WHO WE ARE

Paraclete Press is an ecumenical publisher of books and recordings on Christian spirituality. Our publishing represents a full expression of Christian belief and practice—from Catholic to Evangelical, from Protestant to Orthodox.

Paraclete Press is the publishing arm of the Community of Jesus, an ecumenical monastic community in the Benedictine tradition. As such, we are uniquely positioned in the marketplace without connection to a large corporation and with informal relationships to many branches and denominations of faith.

We like it best when people buy our books from booksellers, our partners in successfully reaching as wide an audience as possible.

WHAT WE ARE DOING

Books

Paraclete Press publishes books that show the richness and depth of what it means to be Christian. Although Benedictine spirituality is at the heart of all that we do, we publish books that reflect the Christian experience across many cultures, time periods, and houses of worship.

We publish books that nourish the vibrant life of the church and its people—books about spiritual practice, formation, history, ideas, and customs.

We have several different series of books within Paraclete Press, including the best-selling Living Library series of modernized classic texts; A Voice from the Monastery—giving voice to men and women monastics about what it means to live a spiritual life today; award-winning literary faith fiction; and books that explore Judaism and Islam and discover how these faiths inform Christian thought and practice.

Recordings

From Gregorian chant to contemporary American choral works, our music recordings celebrate the richness of sacred choral music through the centuries. Paraclete is proud to distribute the recordings of the internationally acclaimed choir Gloriæ Dei Cantores, who have been praised for their "rapt and fathomless spiritual intensity" by American Record Guide, and the Gloriæ Dei Cantores Schola, which specializes in the study and performance of Gregorian chant. Paraclete is also the exclusive North American distributor of the recordings of the Monastic Choir of St. Peter's Abbey in Solesmes, France, long considered to be a leading authority on Gregorian chant performance.

Learn more about us at our Web site: www.paracletepress.com,
or call us toll-free at 1-800-451-5006.

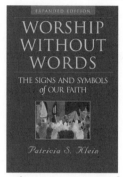

WORSHIP WITHOUT WORDS
Patricia S. Klein

ISBN: 978-1-55725-404-4
255 pages
$19.95, Paperback

IF YOU ARE NEW TO LITURGICAL WORSHIP, through conversion or rediscovery, you may find yourself surrounded by image and traditions that are totally foreign to your experience of church. This thorough guide uses understandable language to explain the signs, symbols, gestures, vestments, and other elements of the liturgy.

PRAYING IN COLOR
Sybil MacBeth

ISBN: 978-1-55725-512-9
103 pages
$16.95, Paperback

MAYBE YOU LOVE COLOR. Maybe you hunger to know God better. Maybe you are a visual or kinesthetic learner, a distractible or impatient soul, or a word-weary pray-er. This new prayer form can take as little or as much time as you have or want to commit. Drawing is half the prayer, the other half is transporting the visual memories or actual images with you to pray throughout the day. *Praying in Color* will forever change the way that you pray.